MOCHI MAGIC

T0023245

MOCHI MAGIC

50 Traditional and Modern Recipes for the Japanese Treat

Kaori Becker

Storey Publishing

The mission of Storey Publishing is to serve our customers by publishing practical information that encourages personal independence in harmony with the environment.

EDITED BY Liz Bevilacqua and Sarah Guare
ART DIRECTION AND BOOK DESIGN BY Carolyn Eckert
TEXT PRODUCTION BY Jennifer Jepson Smith
INDEXED BY Christine R. Lindemer, Boston Road Communications

COVER AND INTERIOR PHOTOGRAPHY BY © Nordeck Photography, Inc.
ADDITIONAL PHOTOGRAPHY BY Kaori Becker, 7, 45, 55, 58, 78, 155, 159
FOOD STYLING BY Jeffrey Larsen and Koka Yamamoto (mochi animals)
ILLUSTRATIONS BY © Andrea Kang

TEXT © 2020 BY KAORI BECKER

All rights reserved. No part of this book may be reproduced without written permission from the publisher, except by a reviewer who may quote brief passages or reproduce illustrations in a review with appropriate credits; nor may any part of this book be reproduced, stored in a retrieval system, or transmitted in any form or by any means — electronic, mechanical, photo-copying, recording, or other — without written permission from the publisher.

The information in this book is true and complete to the best of our knowledge. All recommendations are made without guarantee on the part of the author or Storey Publishing. The author and pub-lisher disclaim any liability in connection with the use of this information.

Storey Publishing
210 MASS MoCA Way
North Adams, MA 01247
storey.com

Printed in China through World Print
10 9 8 7 6 5 4 3 2 1

Library of Congress Cataloging-in-Publication Data on file

Storey books are available at special discounts when purchased in bulk for premiums and sales promotions as well as for fund-raising or educational use. Special editions or book excerpts can also be created to specification. For details, please call 800-827-8673, or send an email to sales@storey.com.

DEDICATED TO
my mother, Yukiko Zinke,
and all of my Japanese ancestors

CONTENTS

A LIFE AND LOVE IN MOCHI

MY JOB IS MADE OF RICE, SUGAR, WATER, AND LOVE.

I am a mochi maker, following in the footsteps of my mother, Yukiko, who showed me how to make mochi during my college years. Together, my mother and I have taught the art of mochi making to guests from all over the world in our cozy home kitchen in the Bay Area. We've created easy and delicious mochi recipes to the delight and wonder of our guests, family, and friends. Through teaching and making, we have realized that the process of making mochi is a process of love. By that, we mean that the act of making mochi brings people together.

Every step in mochi making — the mixing, the steaming, the pounding, and especially the filling process — is an activity that brings out stories, jokes, and smiles. When you're sitting around a table using your hands to make mochi (or play with it!) and breathing in the aromatic scent of cooked rice, sugar, and sweet red bean paste, you can relax and become a child again. When you tap into your inner child, you let your guard down and have fun. In between bites of sweet mochi, you never know what stories and memories will arise, followed by reassuring smiles and heaps of laughter. Guests in our mochi classes have entered our kitchen with a nervous spirit and have left joyful, grateful, and uplifted through making mochi with others. They get to know the other people at the table, and often leave feeling more connected and trusting of people who were strangers just hours before.

Making mochi is as much about creating community as it is about creating food.

WAIT . . . WHAT IS MOCHI?

Mochi is a form of sticky rice cake made from Japanese short-grain rice called *mochigome*. Mochigome is a satisfyingly chewy, sticky rice that is naturally sweeter than ordinary table rice. Mochi itself is neutral in flavor and can be enjoyed in a variety of dishes. It can be eaten on its own with soy sauce, or it can be sweetened and filled with sweet fillings. Mochi flour can also be used in classic desserts, such as brownies and donuts, lending them a unique, chewy texture. Mochi continues to appear in the dishes of many countries besides Japan, and its popularity is ever increasing.

Mochi has been held in high regard within Japanese culture for generations, with rice itself being revered as the "gift of the gods" and considered an omen of good fortune. These little cakes were first enjoyed exclusively by the emperor and nobles, but they were later used as religious offerings to the gods in Shinto rituals. With time, this auspicious delight became an integral part of the Japanese New Year, Girl's Day, and Children's Day celebrations, as well as enjoyed in households throughout Japan both for festive occasions and as a treat in everyday life.

Mochi has an incredibly long and rich history in Japan, but it's hard to know exactly when it was first created, and by whom. The earliest hint comes from steaming tools archaeologists uncovered, similar to those used for mochi making, which date back to the Kofun period (250 to 538 CE).

Plain mochi is consumed most often by Japanese people at the start of each new year. Every new year, Japanese families will place *kagami* mochi (a large mochi cake topped with a small mochi cake and a citrus called a *daidai*) on an alter to bring good fortune. For centuries, Japan has depended on the annual rice harvest as its main source of food, so making mochi at the start of the year represents bringing good luck into the new year, both in harvest and in life. Traditionally, farmers offered mochi to Shinto gods as a gift, to celebrate the rice spirit's arrival. Farmers would recite prayers and give offerings for a successful rice harvest for the coming year. It is believed that giving mochi to others brings good luck upon the giver's household, family, and daily life, and it brings good fortune to the receiver of the mochi as well.

Inadama is the soul or spirit of rice. According to Japanese culture, each grain of rice has a soul, and rice is alive in its hull. Japanese people believe that mochi's inadama can revive and fortify those who eat it. In the past, mochi was given to women after childbirth to strengthen their bodies and help them recover. Even in noodle shops today there is a dish called *chikara udon*, or "strength udon," which is a noodle soup that contains large pieces of mochi. Because pounded mochi contains the spirit of rice, it has long been considered to be a source of divine strength, and this idea lives on in modern Japanese society as well.

MY LIFE WITH MOCHI

I grew up eating mochi, and lots of it!

From the huge *daifuku* mochi (mochi stuffed with sweet red bean paste) we would buy from the local Japanese grocery store to the smaller mochi we got for a dollar apiece at church bazaars run by Japanese moms, mochi has always been a delicious source of comfort. I also remember eating mochi while visiting relatives in Japan. I've always loved the smooth, supple, sticky outer layer of rice complemented by the soft or textured red or white bean paste in the middle.

When my mom taught me how to make mochi, I was in graduate school, working toward my English teaching certification, yet I found myself growing more interested in mochi making. I would talk to my mom over the phone about each element of the process. I would ask her to send me step-by-step photos to post on the small blog I had created. Although I had invested so much time, effort, and money in my graduate studies, my heart and mind were inexorably being pulled in another direction. I felt the most joy when I came home to cook in my kitchen. Eventually, cooking became a calling I could no longer ignore.

When I started teaching cooking classes, I advertised a number of topics — including how to make Vietnamese pho and Indian curry — but it was our mochi class that was the most popular. A steady stream of people kept signing up to learn about it. There is no denying that there is something special about mochi!

INFINITE POSSIBILITIES

I'm forever fascinated by mochi's versatility. It offers endless possibilities for fillings, flavors, and cooking methods. Today, mochi is found in many savory and sweet dishes, with a large variety of unique flavorings. The recipes in this book indicate the many ways that mochi is enjoyed in Japan and throughout the world. Traditional mochi pounded from Japanese sticky rice is eaten most commonly during the new year, but this doesn't mean all mochi is consumed only in January. Mochi, in its many varieties — from mochi balls called *odango* to frozen ice cream mochi to filled (daifuku) mochi — is eaten year-round in Japan and other parts of Asia, and around the world. Many people love its texture and delicious taste.

I delight in creating and tasting new mochi flavors in Japan, the United States, and around the world. Indeed, most of my travel to Asian countries is for mochi research (my excuse to binge on mochi!).

The results of my experiments became the recipes that I'm sharing with you. This book features the diverse and mouthwatering flavor combinations and recipes my mother, our cooking assistants, and I have discovered while experimenting, eating, and teaching people about mochi. Savory or sweet, traditional or new — there is something here for everyone!

My first hope with this book is that it motivates you to cook mochi with your family and friends. As you make mochi, more love and connections will be created, jovial conversations will be had, and sweets will be consumed that leave your bellies full. My second hope is that this book encourages you to think about your roots and how you can keep the memories of your family alive through the art of creating and enjoying food together. Finally, I hope you enjoy our recipes, and that you improve upon them, adapt them, and make unique creations of your own.

In life, as with love and mochi, the possibilities are endless!

MOCHI-MAKING BASICS

Mochi has been made in households across Japan and around the world for centuries. You don't need any special equipment to make it. You can purchase special tools to make the process smoother, but I encourage you to first try out the recipes with kitchen implements you already have on hand. Equipment aside, mochi ingredients like *mochiko* (mochi flour) are easy to find at your local grocery store, Asian market, or online. I will walk you through the five methods of making mochi that I use, as well as some tips and tricks for decorating your finished mochi to perfection.

THE INGREDIENTS

Mochi is made from mochi rice (in the case of pounded mochi) or mochi rice flour, water, and sugar (if making dessert mochi). Mochi can also be filled with a variety of flavors, from traditional bean pastes to non-traditional chocolate truffles.

BEAN PASTE FILLINGS

Adzuki beans. These are used to make sweet red bean paste, including *tsubu-an* and *koshi-an*. They are sometimes called azuki, aduki, or red mung beans. They have a characteristically earthy flavor and natural sweetness, which make them the perfect bean for filling mochi. Among the legume family, adzuki beans are the highest in protein and the lowest in fat. Other benefits include high levels of potassium, fiber, B-complex vitamins, and minerals such as iron and zinc. Whole, dried adzuki beans can usually be found at the local Asian store in the dried legumes section, or online.

Tsubu-an and koshi-an. *Tsubu-an* is the coarse version of sweet red bean paste (*anko*), and *koshi-an* is the smooth version. You can buy premade sweet red bean paste at most Asian grocery stores or make your own. The ingredients for sweet red bean paste are simple — adzuki beans, sugar, and water. For tsubu-an, the beans are cooked, then mashed with sugar without ever passing through a blender or sieve. This results in a chunky, almost fudgy texture beloved by many mochi connoisseurs. Some, like me, prefer tsubu-an for the texture it brings to mochi. For koshi-an, the adzuki beans are also cooked, but then they are mashed, blended, and pressed through a fine-mesh sieve before being mixed with sugar. This results in a smooth, velvety paste.

Shiro-an. This sweet white bean paste is made with large lima beans (also known as butter beans), sugar, and water. *Shiro-an* is available commercially, though it may be hard to find. Make your own by following the recipe on page 58.

TSUBU-AN

SHIRO-AN

KOSHI-AN

ADZUKI BEANS

SWEET RICE AND SWEET RICE FLOUR

Sweet rice. This is what makes mochi what it is: a sticky rice cake. In Japanese, this rice is called mochigome, meaning "mochi rice." The Japanese style of sweet rice is a short-grain rice. The grains look more opaque and white compared to regular short-grain Japanese rice. Sweet rice can also be called sticky rice. When cooked and pounded, the grains of this rice start to meld and stick together, becoming one large mass. Found at most Asian grocery stores, this type of rice is used to make the traditional hand-pounded (or machine-pounded) mochi during the new year.

Mochiko. Also known as sweet rice flour, *mochiko* literally translates to "mochi flour" in Japanese. Mochiko is uncooked sweet rice that has been pulverized to a powder. My favorite brand of mochiko is made by Koda Farms, a third-generation Japanese family-owned rice farm in California. Mochiko is the best ingredient to use when making the standard sweet daifuku mochi. Mochiko can be found in Asian grocery stores across North America and online.

Kiri mochi. Several recipes in this book require either home-pounded mochi or a product called *kiri mochi*, which is commercially produced plain pounded mochi cut into solid rectangles. Kiri mochi can be used wherever plain pounded mochi is required — for example, in Yaki Mochi with Sweet Soy Sauce (page 114) and Bacon-Wrapped Mochi (page 116). Kiri mochi is generally sold in bags of individually wrapped rectangles, available at Japanese grocery stores or online. You can also use sprouted brown rice mochi squares in place of kiri mochi.

MOCHIKO

SWEET RICE

DUSTING AND FLAVORING

Matcha. This high-quality green tea, ground into powdered form, comes in two main grades: ceremonial and culinary. Culinary grade is a less vibrant green and tastes more intense, bitter, and grassy compared to the ceremonial grade. Culinary grade matcha is cheaper and can be used in all the recipes; however, I do recommend using ceremonial grade in any recipe where matcha's taste and color really need to shine, such as in the Matcha Syrup (page 171) and the matcha agar cubes in the *anmitsu* recipe (page 138). Reputable brands of matcha include Maeda-en, Matcha Love, and any matcha produced in the city of Uji, Japan (a city known for being a producer of matcha).

Yomogi. This flavoring is made from the leaves of the Japanese mugwort plant (*yomogi*) that have been dried and pulverized. Its taste is slightly similar to matcha but with an earthier, herbier flavor profile. Fresh yomogi is not commonly found in the United States, but you can find the dried version in Japanese grocery stores or online. Yomogi-flavored mochi pairs excellently with a topping of *kinako* powder.

Kinako. Literally translated as "yellow flour," *kinako* is simply roasted soybeans that have been finely ground into a powder. Rolling mochi dough in kinako gives it an earthy, nutty flavor — similar to that of peanut powder — with a beautiful golden hue that many love. You can find kinako in Japanese and Korean grocery stores or online.

Sesame seeds. Sesame seeds add a delicious nuttiness to mochi and work well as mochi toppings. Simply dip mochi in a bowl of water, shake off the excess, and drop the mochi into a generous bowl of black, white, or mixed black and white sesame seeds. Roll the mochi around in the bowl. The seeds adhere to the mochi, for a special, more traditional look.

MATCHA

KINAKO

YOMOGI

SESAME
SEEDS

Katakuriko. Also known as Japanese potato starch, *katakuriko* is used for dusting the mochi as you shape it, preventing the large mochi mass from sticking to your hands and the cutting board. It also allows you to easily shape and form each individual piece of mochi. Katakuriko was once derived from the roots of the dogtooth violet, but nowadays it is made from potatoes. You cannot substitute American brands of potato starch for katakuriko. If you can't find katakuriko, use cornstarch instead.

Agar powder. This ingredient is essential to making kanten, which is a type of Japanese jelly. In fact, *kanten* is the Japanese word for agar, although the term refers to both the ingredient as well as the gelatin-like pudding made with it. Instead of using gelatin to make Jell-O, most Japanese recipes will use agar/kanten powder. Unlike gelatin, agar/kanten is entirely vegan. In addition, it has no taste and is semitranslucent. Also unlike gelatin, it can set at room temperature and produces a firmer texture.

Cornstarch. An alternative to katakuriko used for dusting mochi, cornstarch can be found in any grocery store in the United States. It is not as finely powdered as katakuriko, but it still does a great job. I often use it more than katakuriko because it keeps the mochi drier and less sticky for easy handling, and is also more readily available than katakuriko.

THE TOOLS

A large steamer. Almost any kind of steamer will work when making mochi; there's no need for it to be fancy. We use a stainless steel steamer that consists of two parts: a pot on the bottom and a perforated basket section that sits on top of the pot and lets steam in. A lid on top seals in the steam. You can find steamers at local Asian grocery stores or markets, but basically any kind of steamer can be used to make steamed mochi.

Three-foot square of white cotton cloth with a tight weave. This cloth is a necessary part of steaming mochi. It is placed over the top of the steamer basket to prevent the mochi batter from spilling into the steaming water. You cannot use cheesecloth, as its weave is not fine enough to catch the mochi batter. You can buy cotton cloth, such as muslin, from fabric or kitchen supply stores to make this.

Food-safe disposable gloves. Vinyl, polyethylene, or nitrile (not latex) food-safe gloves are useful if you choose to work with the mochi right out of the steamer or microwave, something we often need to do because it's easier to break off pieces and shape them when the mochi is still quite hot. It's important to find powder-free food-safe vinyl gloves when working with hot mochi.

A large, heavy-duty cutting board, preferably wooden. When we steam mochi, we often make large batches (25 to 30 pieces), which calls for a large cutting board. Wooden boards work best, although a durable, heat-proof plastic board can be used instead, if that's all you have.

Large wooden or metal bowl. You'll need a large bowl for pounding the cooked sticky rice. During *mochitsuki*, the traditional mochi-pounding ceremony, a large, heavy wooden bowl called an *usu* is used for pounding the mochi. However, any large metal or wooden bowl will do the job.

Food-safe wooden or plastic mallet, or a stand mixer with a paddle attachment. If you are making mochi the traditional way, you will need a pounding implement. It's important to find mallets that are not treated with chemicals, and you should be wary of nonwooden mallets in particular, as they may not be food-safe. If you do not have a mallet, you can use a stand mixer with a paddle attachment to pound the mochi instead.

Whisk. A whisk is the best tool for mixing mochi rice flour, sugar, and water together for both steamed and microwaved mochi.

Pastry brush. Use this for brushing off excess cornstarch or potato starch from the tops of your finished mochi. Nothing beats the common household pastry brush.

Cupcake liners (standard size). These baking cups work as the perfect receptacles for holding finished mochi and keeping them from sticking to each other. They also make the finished mochi look fancier, cuter, and ready for gift-giving or presenting at a party.

THE PROCESS

Mochi is a simple yet versatile food that can be prepared in a number of ways. All five mochi-making methods described in this chapter are detailed later in this book, including step-by-step guidance so you'll know exactly how to prepare each mochi dish.

STEAMED MOCHI

Steamed mochi is made using mochiko, water, sugar, and flavorings. The mochi is steamed, then sectioned into pieces and filled. Although there is no real art to the mixing and steaming process, there is definitely technique involved in handling the mochi after it has been steamed. Mochi can be the most pillowy, comforting creature, or it can be an absolute monster! If you don't use enough starch when rolling or folding the mochi, it will stick to your hands and to the cutting board, making it nearly impossible to portion and fill. Fear not! The step-by-step photos in chapter 2 will show you how to handle mochi, and soon you'll be on your way to becoming a mochi master!

MICROWAVED MOCHI

Hands down, microwaving is the easiest and fastest method for cooking mochi. One batch of microwaved mochi takes 10 minutes, whereas steamed mochi will take 40 minutes and pounded mochi will take even longer. I have found through a lot of testing, practice, and teaching that steamed mochi is a bit softer than microwaved mochi, but, frankly, it's not a huge difference. Microwaved mochi can be made softer by adding a bit more liquid to the dough before cooking. After being cooked, microwaved mochi can even be pounded with a mallet or mixed by hand with a rice paddle to soften it further. Most of the time, I microwave mochi because it is a quick dessert for family and friends — and a hit at each potluck I attend. If you, like me, prefer to do things quickly, I highly recommend this method, detailed in chapter 2.

POUNDED MOCHI

Hand-pounded mochi is the most traditional kind and is mainly eaten during the New Year. In a traditional mochitsuki pounding ceremony, a *kine* (a large wooden mallet) is used to beat the rice into a large mass (see the box on page 109 for more about this ceremony). If you cannot find a kine, use a food-safe mallet, which you can buy from the hardware store or online. The Japanese sweet rice is cooked first, then placed in a large wooden or metal bowl and pounded. Alternatively, you could purchase a Japanese mochi machine to do both the steaming and pounding for you. A mochi machine is useful when making very large quantities of plain mochi rice cakes, such as those in Yaki Mochi with Sweet Soy Sauce (page 114). We'll explore these mochi options in chapter 4.

traditional

store bought

Pounded mochi has a denser, stickier texture than dessert mochi made with mochiko. During the New Year, my mother and her friend Emiko prepare this kind of mochi to go with traditional *ozoni*, a light soup containing chicken stock, *dashi*, shiitake mushrooms, chicken, daikon, carrots, and soy sauce (you'll find my version on page 119). Large pieces of pounded mochi are reheated in hot simmering water, then placed into a bowl of the soup. It is a delectable experience watching the mochi become softer and softer in the soup. When lifted by a pair of chopsticks, the mochi stretches, similar to the way mozzarella cheese stretches when a slice of pizza is lifted from the whole, hot pie. The light yet flavorful chicken stock combined with chewy, stretchy mochi is a match made in heaven.

BOILED MOCHI

Boiling mochi is mainly reserved for dishes involving odango, which are mochi balls often skewered on a stick and slathered in a sauce, such as Mitarashi Dango (page 128), or added to soups, where the mochi balls look like round rice dumplings surrounded by an earthy, sweet soup of red bean paste and water. We'll explore the joys of odango in chapter 6.

BAKED MOCHI

Baked mochi is probably the least traditional kind of mochi, at least in Japan. Japanese families rarely bake, and many Japanese kitchens do not even have an oven. Baked desserts are purchased at the local bakery. Hawaii has been a front-runner in the creation of baked mochi, inspiring many similar treats around the world. *Chi chi dango*, for example, is a popular baked mochi dish in Hawaii. I believe that baked mochi exemplifies how adaptable mochi is. No longer something that is simply steamed or pounded, mochi can be mixed with various flavorings, milk, eggs, and oil to make unique mochi cakes, brownies, and more. Turn to chapter 7 for more about these treats.

KURI MANJU
(page 143)

Daifuku (Filled) Mochi:
THE DOUGH

Daifuku mochi refers to mochi that have some kind of sweet filling. *Daifuku* literally translates to "great luck" or "big luck" because daifuku mochi is believed to bring good luck to the giver and receiver of this mochi. This chapter covers the outside portion of daifuku, which is the mochi, and not the daifuku filling. You will need to prepare your fillings (see chapter 3) *before* you make the dough, however, because the dough needs to be filled very quickly while it is still warm. You'll need a microwave or a steamer to make the dough. *Note:* Any microwaved daifuku mochi recipe in this book can be steamed instead of microwaved, using the same ratio of ingredients.

DAIFUKU Q & A

Q: **Does daifuku mochi need to have a filling?**
A: Yes, all daifuku mochi have some type of sweet filling. The flavor from daifuku mochi mainly comes from the filling of the mochi, not from the outer mochi layer. Therefore, having a filling is essential.

Q: **Is there a difference in consistency between steamed mochi and microwaved mochi?**
A: Yes. Microwaved mochi is a little chewier and firmer than steamed mochi because some of the water evaporates in the microwave. Steamed mochi stays moister and is therefore a bit softer, but to be honest, the difference is slight. Microwaved mochi is much faster to make, easier to handle, and easier to clean up afterward, so my mom and I almost always prefer to use the microwave method, especially if we are short on time. Steaming is great if you are making large batches of mochi, such as 25 mochi at a time. The microwave is best if making smaller quantities — recipes using up to 2 cups of mochiko.

Q: **Does mochi need to be hot when you work with it?**
A: Yes. The cooler the mochi gets, the firmer and less pliable it becomes, making it difficult to pinch filling into the inside of the mochi. After heating, you have 10 to 15 minutes to fill the mochi while it is still warm. However, you don't want to burn your hands! To solve this problem, wear food-safe vinyl gloves, or wait about 5 minutes for the mochi to cool down before parceling it into pieces and filling each piece.

Q: Are daifuku mochi hard to fill?

A: This is a tricky question to answer. Filling the mochi takes a little practice initially, and at the beginning you may be slow. But after you've made mochi a few times, the skill is pretty easy to pick up. You will get faster and faster and develop your own technique, depending on what is most comfortable for your hands. This book shows one filling style to get you started, but after you have mastered our style, feel free to try your own.

Q: How large should I make my mochi pieces?

A: This is up to you. You may want to make small mochi that are easier to eat. Generally, I make mochi 2½ to 3 inches in diameter. In the beginning, it may be difficult to form uniformly sized mochi. Indeed, this is challenging even for advanced mochi makers. However, with practice and muscle memory, all your mochi may start to have the same size and look.

STEAMED WHITE DAIFUKU MOCHI

Steamed daifuku mochi is typically served in traditional Japanese mochi shops. For fillings, choose red or white bean paste (pages 56 and 58), Matcha Truffle (page 78), or Chocolate and Peanut Butter (page 75) — the possibilities are endless! You'll need a double-decker Asian steamer and a three-foot square of white cotton cloth with a tight weave (page 18).

INGREDIENTS

3 cups mochiko

1½ cups sugar

3 cups water

2 cups cornstarch or Japanese potato starch, for dusting

1 cup filling of choice

NOTE: To make different flavors, mix 3 teaspoons matcha or other powdered or liquid flavoring of choice into the batter.

YIELD:
24
PIECES

DIRECTIONS

1. Add enough water to the steamer base to fill the pot halfway (make sure the water doesn't touch the steaming basket). Bring the water to a boil over medium-high heat.

2. While the water heats, mix together the mochiko and sugar with a whisk or spatula until incorporated, about 1 minute. Add the water and mix until the water is fully incorporated. You shouldn't see any lumps, and the mixture should look smooth, like pancake batter.

3. Thoroughly wet the cotton cloth with water, then wring it out. Drape the cloth over the steaming basket of the steamer. Pour the mochi mixture on top of the cloth (3A). Put the lid on the steamer and rest the excess cloth on top of the steamer lid so it doesn't hang down the side of the pot (3B).

4. Steam over medium-high heat until the mochi is solid, thick, uniformly glossy, and easy to peel from the cloth, 25 to 40 minutes. Replenish the steamer base with additional hot water as needed. To test if the mochi is done, mix it with a spatula. If it is all the same color and texture, it is done.

Recipe continues on page 30

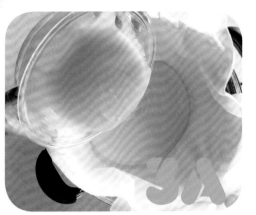

daifuku (filled) mochi: the dough   29

5. Rub a large cutting board with ½ cup of the cornstarch, focusing on the middle section of the board where the cooked mochi dough will be placed. When the mochi is done steaming, lift the cloth from the steamer by the corners and carry it to the cutting board. Peel the mochi off the cloth and transfer it to the center of the cutting board. The mochi should peel off easily. If not, use a spatula to get the mochi off the cloth and onto the board. Let cool for 5 minutes.

6. Coat your hands with plenty of cornstarch. If the mochi is still hot, you can slip on gloves before dusting your hands with the starch. Sprinkle a healthy amount of cornstarch over the mochi mass. Carefully slide your fingers under one side of the mochi and roll it over on the cutting board to coat the mass entirely in starch.

7. Form the mochi into a log 4 to 5 inches wide. Using your nondominant hand (the hand you don't write with), grab a golf ball–sized piece of mochi and pinch the piece off from the mass by curling your index finger and your thumb together. At the same time, pull the pinched mochi piece away from the mass with your dominant hand.

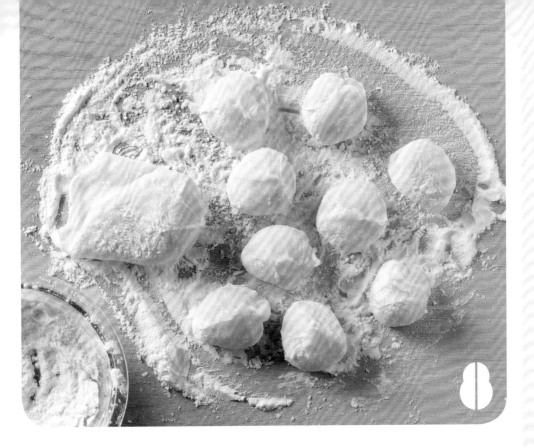

8. Cover this piece with starch and lay it on the board. Repeat until the whole mound has been used.

9. Fill each mochi following the directions that start on page 32.

10. Cover a plate in cornstarch or set out 24 cupcake liners. Round each mochi with your hands a few times, then set them on the cornstarch-covered plate or in the cupcake liners. Enjoy immediately or store at room temperature for up to 1 day or in an airtight container in the freezer for up to 1 month (defrost for 3 hours before eating).

1. Slightly flatten a mochi piece into a circle about ¾-inch thick.

2. Roll 1 rounded teaspoon of filling into a ball and place it in the center of the mochi.

3. Cover your hands with cornstarch. Starting at 3 and 9 o'clock on the circle, fold the edges of the mochi together over the filling, pinching tightly so they stick together.

Recipe continues on next page

4. Pinch together the opposing sides, 12 and 6 o'clock, to form a loose bundle.

5. Finally, pinch all the corners into the center of the mochi, making sure to pinch hard enough to seal.

6. Flip the mochi upside down and brush off excess starch. Repeat with the remaining mochi pieces. Enjoy!

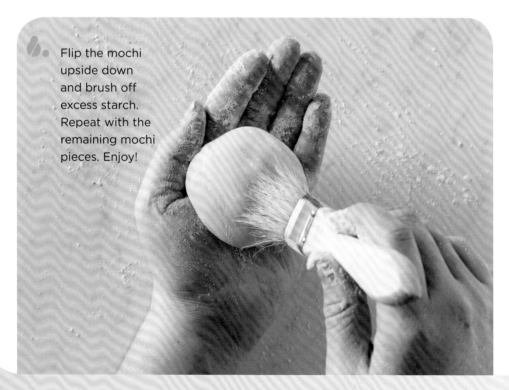

MICROWAVED WHITE DAIFUKU MOCHI

I love this style of mochi because it takes only 15 to 20 minutes from start to finish, and the result is just as delicious as steaming your own mochi dough! This is the basic, go-to recipe my mom and I turn to when we are crunched for time. For fillings, choose sweet red bean paste (page 56), chocolate truffle (page 76), or fresh fruit. It helps to round the paste or truffle filling into one-inch balls in advance so you can assemble the mochi easily. The recipe can easily be doubled — just be sure to increase the microwave time by 2 minutes in steps 2 and 4.

INGREDIENTS

1 cup mochiko

½ cup sugar

1¼ cups water

½ cup cornstarch or Japanese potato starch, for dusting

½ cup filling of choice

DIRECTIONS

1. Whisk together the mochiko and sugar in a microwavable bowl. Add the water and mix until the water is fully incorporated. You shouldn't see any lumps, and the mixture should look smooth, like pancake batter.

2. Microwave, uncovered, on high for 2 minutes.

3. Dip a spatula in water and use it to stir the mochi dough. The dough should be sticky, thick, and starting to look glossy. Mix well so that the dough heats evenly and almost all the dough becomes the same color.

4. Microwave the mixture for 2 minutes longer.

5. Remove the mochi mixture from the microwave and stir well with the spatula.

6. Rub a large cutting board with the cornstarch, focusing on the middle section of the board where the cooked mochi dough will be placed. Transfer the mochi to the center of the board. Let cool for 5 minutes.

Recipe continues on next page

YIELD:
5-7
PIECES

7. Lightly rub the cornstarch over the top of the mochi. Carefully roll the mochi into an approximately 3-inch-wide, 10-inch-long log, with all sides adequately covered with cornstarch. If the mochi is still hot, use gloves or wait 5 more minutes for it to cool. Pinch off golf ball–sized pieces from the mochi mass, dusting each piece with starch as you go, until the whole mound is used.

8. Fill each mochi with a filling of your choice (see the filling instructions starting on page 33). Cover a plate in cornstarch or set out 5 to 7 cupcake liners. Round each mochi with your hands a few times, then set them on the cornstarch-covered plate or in the cupcake liners. Enjoy immediately or store at room temperature for up to 1 day or in the freezer for up to 1 month (defrost for 3 hours before eating).

NUTELLA AND STRAWBERRIES MOCHI

NOTE: It's essential to refrigerate the Nutella that you'll be using for the filling for at least 3 hours in advance; otherwise it will be too gooey to scoop out and form the mochi around.

INGREDIENTS

1 cup mochiko

1 cup water

¼ cup Nutella, at room temperature

Cornstarch or Japanese potato starch, for dusting

1 (13-ounce) container refrigerated Nutella (see note)

5 strawberries, cut into ½-inch horizontal discs

YIELD:
10
PIECES

You need only four ingredients to make this recipe: Nutella spread, strawberries, sugar, and mochiko! Nutella's chocolate-hazelnut flavor infuses into the outer layer of mochi as well as the mochi filling. The strawberries add a fresh note and cut the sweetness of the Nutella with a little acidity, but you can omit the berries, if you prefer.

DIRECTIONS

1. Whisk together the mochiko, water, and ¼ cup room-temperature Nutella in a microwavable bowl until thoroughly incorporated.

2. Microwave on high, uncovered, for 2 minutes. Remove from the microwave with a baking mitt (it will be hot!), and stir the mixture with a spatula until it has an even, gooey consistency. Microwave again for 2 minutes, and stir again until it has an even consistency.

3. Dust a large cutting board with plenty of cornstarch. Transfer the mochi to the board. Coat the top of the mochi and your hands with cornstarch, then roll the mochi into an approximately 3-inch-wide log, with all sides adequately covered with cornstarch. Allow to cool for 5 minutes. If the mochi is still hot, use gloves or wait 5 more minutes for it to cool. Pinch off 10 pieces from the mochi mass and flatten each piece into a ½ inch disk.

4. Working with one mochi at a time, place a sliced round disk of strawberry on the mochi, then spoon ½ teaspoon of the chilled spread on the strawberry. Pinch the mochi to seal, flip it over, and round with your hands. Repeat with the remaining pieces. Enjoy immediately or store at room temperature for up to 1 day.

MATCHA MOCHI

Matcha mochi is a big hit in our mochi classes: Most partici-
pants say it's their favorite kind. I recommend using organic
matcha from a reputable company like Maeda-en or Matcha
Love, produced in Japan. Try filling with sweet red bean paste
(page 56) with or without fresh fruit or green tea ice cream.
It helps to round paste filling into one-inch balls in advance
so you can assemble the mochi easily. The recipe can be
doubled — just be sure to increase the microwave time by
2 minutes in steps 2 and 4.

INGREDIENTS

- 1 **cup mochiko**
- ½ **cup sugar**
- 1 **teaspoon good-quality matcha, sifted**
- 1¼ **cups water**
- 1 **cup cornstarch or Japanese potato starch, for dusting**
- ½ **cup filling of choice**

DIRECTIONS

1. Whisk together the mochiko, sugar, and matcha in a microwavable bowl. Add the water and mix until the water is fully incorporated. You shouldn't see any lumps, and the mixture should look smooth, like pancake batter.

2. Microwave, uncovered, on high for 2 minutes.

3. Dip a spatula in water and use it to stir the mochi dough. The dough should be sticky, thick, and starting to look partially glossy. Mix well so that the dough heats evenly and almost all of the dough becomes the same color.

4. Microwave for 2 minutes longer. Remove the mixture from the microwave and stir well with the spatula.

5. Rub a large cutting board with ½ cup of the cornstarch, focusing on the middle section of the board where the cooked mochi dough will be placed. Transfer the mochi to the center of the board. Let cool for 5 minutes.

YIELD:
7-8
PIECES

Recipe continues on next page

6. Lightly rub the some of the cornstarch over the top of the mochi. Carefully roll the mochi into an approximately 3-inch-wide, 10-inch-long log, with all sides adequately covered with cornstarch. If the mochi is still hot, use gloves or wait 5 more minutes for it to cool. Pinch off golf ball–sized pieces from the mochi mass, dusting each piece with cornstarch as you go, until the whole mound is used.

7. Fill each mochi with a filling of your choice (see the filling instructions starting on page 33). Enjoy immediately or store at room temperature for up to 1 day or in the freezer for up to 1 month (defrost for 3 hours before eating).

VARIATION: For **Yomogi Mochi**, *replace the matcha with 2 teaspoons yomogi powder, and use kinako for dusting instead of cornstarch.*

CHOCOLATE MOCHI

Chocolaty and oh so soft, this mochi makes a great outer layer for various fillings, including red or white bean paste (pages 56 and 58), Chocolate and Peanut Butter (page 75), Nutella, or Chocolate Truffle (page 76). This recipe is easy to make because the main ingredients are simply chocolate chips and mochiko. If you are using paste or truffles for filling, it helps to round that filling into one-inch balls in advance so that you can assemble the mochi easily. The recipe can be easily doubled — just be sure to increase the microwave time by 3 minutes in step 2 and 2 minutes in step 4.

INGREDIENTS

1 cup mochiko

½ cup sugar

⅓ cup milk chocolate chips

1¼ cup water

Cornstarch or Japanese potato starch, for dusting

½ cup filling of choice

Cocoa powder, for dusting top of mochi (optional)

YIELD:
7-8
PIECES

DIRECTIONS

1. Whisk together the mochiko, sugar, and chocolate chips in a microwavable bowl. Add the water and stir well until mochiko is smooth. It's okay if there are chunks of chocolate — these will melt in the microwave.

2. Microwave, uncovered, on high for 2 minutes.

3. Dip a spatula in water and use it to fold the mochi dough until it is consistent in texture. Mix well so that almost all of the dough becomes the same color.

4. Microwave the mixture for 2 minutes longer, then stir well with the spatula.

5. Cover your cutting board with lots of cornstarch, spreading it lightly with your fingers. Transfer the mochi to the board, then generously sprinkle cornstarch on top of the mochi mass. Let cool for 5 minutes.

Recipe continues on next page

6. Lightly rub the cornstarch over the top of the mochi. Carefully roll the mochi into a 3-inch-wide, 10-inch-long log, with all sides adequately covered with cornstarch. If the mochi is still hot, use gloves or wait 5 more minutes for it to cool. Pinch off golf ball–sized pieces from the mochi mass, dusting each piece with starch as you go, until the whole mound is used.

7. After separating all pieces, fill each mochi with a filling of your choice. Enjoy immediately or store at room temperature for up to 1 day or in the freezer for up to 1 month (defrost for 3 hours before eating).

VARIATION: *Substitute 2 teaspoons of vanilla extract for the chocolate chips to make vanilla-flavored mochi. Try it with a Matcha Truffle Filling (page 78) inside, if desired.*

JAPANESE PLUM WINE MOCHI

This mochi carries the delicious sweet flavor of plum wine, but the alcohol is cooked out of it. The result is a light pink mochi that tastes of plum wine — a special treat. I suggest filling this mochi with sweet red bean paste (page 56). It helps to round fillings into one-inch balls and chill ahead of time, so that you can assemble the mochi easily. The recipe can be easily doubled — just be sure to increase the microwave time by 2 minutes at each step.

INGREDIENTS

1 cup mochiko

½ cup sugar

¾ cup Japanese plum wine (see note)

⅓ cup water

Cornstarch or Japanese potato starch, for dusting

½ cup filling of choice

> **NOTE:** For best results, use Hakutsuru or Kikkoman brand plum wine.

YIELD:
7-8
PIECES

DIRECTIONS

1. Whisk together the mochiko and sugar in a medium microwavable bowl. Add the wine and water, then whisk well, making sure no lumps remain and the mixture is fully incorporated.

2. Microwave, uncovered, on high for 2 minutes.

3. Dip a spatula in water and use it to stir the mochi dough. The dough should be sticky, thick, and starting to look more glossy. Mix well so that the dough heats evenly and almost all of the dough becomes the same color.

4. Microwave the mixture for 2 minutes longer, then stir well with the spatula.

5. Cover a large cutting board with lots of cornstarch, spreading it around lightly with your fingers. Transfer the mochi to the board, then generously sprinkle cornstarch over the mochi mass. Let cool for 5 minutes.

6. Lightly rub the cornstarch over the top of the mochi. Carefully roll the mochi into an approximately 3-inch-wide, 10-inch-long log, with all sides adequately covered with cornstarch. If the mochi is still hot, use gloves or wait 5 more minutes for it to cool. Pinch off golf ball–sized pieces from the mochi mass until the whole mound is used.

7. Fill each mochi with 2 teaspoons of bean paste. Enjoy immediately or store at room temperature for up to 1 day or in the freezer for up to 1 month (defrost for 3 hours before eating).

ROSEWATER MOCHI

I love the delicate flavor rose water adds to desserts. This mochi is very popular in our classes, and the rose flavor pairs well with the earthy-sweet red bean paste. Rose water can be a strong flavor, so use a little bit at first and experiment with different levels to suit your taste. I suggest filling the mochi with sweet white bean paste (page 58) mixed with ½ teaspoon rose water, Strawberry–Rose Truffle Filling (page 82), sweet red bean paste (page 56) with fresh strawberries, or white chocolate chips with fresh strawberries.

INGREDIENTS

- 1 **cup mochiko**
- ½ **cup sugar**
- 1¼ **cups water**
- 1 **teaspoon rose water, such as Cortas brand**
- 1 **drop liquid red food coloring or ¼ teaspoon food-grade beet powder**
- **Cornstarch or Japanese potato starch, for dusting**
- ½ **cup filling of choice**

DIRECTIONS

1. Whisk together the mochiko, sugar, water, rose water, and food coloring in a large microwavable bowl, stirring until no lumps remain and the mixture is fully incorporated.

2. Microwave, uncovered, on high for 2 minutes. Dip a spatula in water and use it to stir the mixture until fully mixed, about 2 minutes.

3. Microwave again for 2 minutes, then stir until evenly incorporated. The mixture should look pink and glossy compared to the opaque batter it used to be.

4. Rub a large cutting board with cornstarch, focusing on the middle section of the board where the cooked mochi dough will be placed. Transfer the mochi to the center of the board. Let cool for 5 minutes.

5. Lightly rub the some of the cornstarch over the top of the mochi. Carefully roll the mochi into an approximately 3-inch-wide log, with all sides adequately covered with cornstarch. If the mochi is still hot, use gloves or wait 5 more minutes for it to cool. Pinch off 7 or 8 equal-sized pieces, dusting each piece with cornstarch as you go.

YIELD:
7-8
PIECES

6. Fill each mochi with a filling of your choice (see the filling instructions starting on page 33). Use plenty of cornstarch while working to prevent the mochi from sticking to your hands. Enjoy immediately or store at room temperature for up to 1 day or in the freezer for up to 1 month (defrost for 3 hours before eating).

COCONUT MOCHI

Coconut mochi is simply delicious and addicting. Even if you don't like coconut, I highly recommend this mochi flavor. Many times, I can even eat this without a filling — that's how good it is. I recommend filling it with Haupia Pudding (page 66), Nutella, or sweet red bean paste (page 56). Family and friends will surely be wanting more!

INGREDIENTS

1 (13.5-ounce) can full-fat coconut milk

2 cups mochiko

1 cup sugar

½ cup water

Cornstarch or Japanese potato starch, for dusting

1 cup filling of choice

Unsweetened coconut flakes, for coating (optional)

DIRECTIONS

1. Whisk together the coconut milk, mochiko, and sugar in a large microwavable bowl until combined. Whisking constantly, add the water in a steady stream until the mixture is about the consistency of pancake batter and no lumps remain.

2. Microwave, uncovered, on high for 2 minutes. Stir the mixture with a spatula until well mixed.

3. Microwave until the mochi becomes a thick, glossy mass, about 2 minutes.

4. Cover a large cutting board with ¼ cup cornstarch, spreading it around lightly with your fingers. Transfer the mochi to the board. Let cool for 5 minutes.

5. Generously sprinkle cornstarch over the mochi mass. Carefully roll the mochi into an approximately 3-inch-wide, 10-inch-long log, with all sides adequately covered with cornstarch. If the mochi is still hot, use gloves or wait 5 more minutes for it to cool. Pinch off golf ball–sized pieces from the mochi mass until the whole mound is used.

6. Fill each mochi with a haupia square and pinch to seal (see the filling instructions starting on page 33).

YIELD:
12-15
PIECES

If desired, pour the coconut into a medium bowl, and fill a separate medium bowl with water. Submerge one piece of filled mochi in the water, moistening all sides, then roll the mochi in the coconut until coated. Repeat with the remaining mochi for a beautiful look.

MANGO MOCHI WITH FRESH MANGO

Fresh, ripe mango is an excellent filling for mochi. When you bite into it, you are immediately greeted by a burst of mango juice and flesh. Make sure to use mango that is ripe enough to be meaty and taste sweet but not so ripe that it disintegrates. Ripe is always better than underripe, as it will deliver a sweet mango taste. If the mango is ripe and sweet enough, you could even omit the sweet bean paste.

INGREDIENTS

1 cup mochiko

¼ cup sugar

¾ cup mango juice

⅓ cup water

Cornstarch or Japanese potato starch, for dusting

1 fresh ripe mango, cut into 1-inch squares

½ cup sweet red or white bean paste (pages 56 and 58)

DIRECTIONS

1. Whisk together the mochiko and sugar in a medium microwavable bowl. Add the mango juice and water, and whisk until even in consistency. The mixture should look light orange, opaque, and similar to a pancake batter.

2. Microwave, uncovered, for 2 minutes. Stir and fold the mixture with a spatula until even in consistency.

3. Microwave for 2 minutes, then stir and fold again until even in consistency. The mochi should look more glossy and become one sticky mass.

4. Dust a cutting board with cornstarch. Transfer the mochi mixture to the board, then dust the top with cornstarch, making sure the entire mass is covered. Allow to cool for 5 minutes. Carefully roll the mochi into an approximately 3-inch-wide log, with all sides adequately covered with cornstarch. If the mochi is still hot, use gloves or wait 5 more minutes for it to cool. Pinch off 2-inch-diameter pieces from the mass until the whole mound is used.

YIELD:
5-6
MOCHI

5. Fill each piece with a square of mango and 1 teaspoon of sweet bean paste, then seal. Enjoy while still warm or cooled to room temperature. Eat this mochi the same day you make it, as the fruit will go bad the next day. Do not refrigerate, or the mochi may become hard.

MAKING JUICE-INFUSED MOCHI DOUGH

Add fruit juice, such as passion fruit, guava, or pineapple, to mochi to easily color it and create unique mochi flavors. Use these ratios when adding fruit juice to mochi:

	MOCHIKO	SUGAR	WATER	FRUIT JUICE
5–7 mochi	1 cup	¼ cup	⅓ cup	¾ cup
12–14 mochi	2 cups	½ cup	⅔ cup	1½ cups
21–24 mochi	3 cups	¾ cup	1 cup	3 cups

YOMOGI MOCHI (page 40) with
SWEET RED BEAN PASTE (page 56)

3

Daifuku (Filled) Mochi: THE FILLINGS

Before you make daifuku mochi dough, you must prepare the fillings. That's because once the mochi dough is steamed or microwaved, you need to work quickly to fill the mochi while it is warm and pliable. Some fillings, such as the traditional bean paste (unless store-bought), are more time intensive than others that rely on easy-to-use ingredients such as fresh fruit and Nutella. The fillings range from traditional to more modern twists on Asian and American flavors. I encourage you to experiment with creating your own unique fillings as well.

MOCHI FILLINGS Q & A

Q: Do certain fillings require specific techniques and temperatures to help with the filling process?

A: Yes. Some fillings, such as peanut butter or sweet red bean paste, are thicker and can be used at room temperature. Others melt quickly — like those involving Nutella, jam, or truffles — and are easier to use when pre-chilled in the freezer or refrigerator. For example, Nutella at room temperature is liquidy; refrigerate it and it hardens to the consistency of peanut butter. At this point, you can scoop it, form it into balls, and freeze the balls. Freezing any kind of filling as balls makes the filling process easier and cleaner: You won't have filling dripping and melting while you assemble the mochi. Fillings can also be frozen in ice cube tray sections if that is easier for you than rolling them into balls.

Q: Can you freeze all of the fillings in this chapter?

A: The only exceptions to freezing would be puddings and fresh fruit. These two types of fillings can be refrigerated, but they tend to taste different or have a less desirable texture once frozen and thawed in hot mochi. Otherwise, the freezing method works well for generally any kind of paste: bean pastes, taro paste, peanut butter, Nutella, and truffles.

Q: What kind of white chocolate should I use for the flavored truffles?

A: It is imperative to use a good-quality white chocolate. If you do not, the truffle will not come together; it will separate into butter and white milk solids. I use Ghirardelli Classic White baking chips, but you can use Guittard white chocolate chips or any high-quality white chocolate that comes in bars. If you use bar chocolate instead of chips, weigh the bar to make sure it matches the weight indicated in the recipe.

Q: Can I get creative with my white chocolate truffle flavors?

A: Absolutely yes! I've used almond extract and vanilla extract, among others, to flavor the truffles (add ½ teaspoon of any kind of extract per cup of white chocolate chips). Lavender extract could also go very well with any white truffle flavor; simply leave out the matcha or other flavoring component, and add the extract instead.

Q: Should the truffles be refrigerated when I am ready to fill my mochi?

A: It's up to you. If you like hot, oozing chocolate, I recommend keeping the truffles at room temperature and eating the mochi 1 minute after they are wrapped. But if you prefer firmer chocolate or just want to save these treats for later, you can use truffle balls directly out of the refrigerator and wrap hot mochi around them. They will melt a bit when being wrapped, but when they return to room temperature, they will firm up again.

TRADITIONAL FILLINGS

TSUBU-AN AND KOSHI-AN
(SWEET RED BEAN PASTE)

Making your own sweet red bean paste, or *an*, does take a bit of time, but is a lot easier than you might think! After the beans soak overnight, all you need to do is employ a watchful eye while they cook, so it is simple to make a large batch. You'll need a food processor or blender for this recipe. You can make this paste coarse (tsubu-an) or smooth (koshi-an), depending on whether you choose to purée the beans or not. You will need to soak the beans overnight, so plan ahead.

INGREDIENTS

2 **cups dried adzuki beans**

5 **cups boiling water**

2 **cups sugar**

¼ **teaspoon salt**

YIELD:
ABOUT **2 ½** CUPS (FOR **24** BALLS)

DIRECTIONS

1. The day before you plan to make the paste, place the beans in a large heatproof bowl and pour in enough of the boiling water to cover the beans by 3 inches. Let soak overnight.

2. The next day, drain the beans and transfer them to a large pot. Add enough water to cover the beans by 2 inches. Bring to a boil over high heat, and cook for 5 minutes. You will see a lot of foam coming up.

3. Drain and rinse the beans in a colander or sieve. Rinse the pot, return the beans, and add enough water to cover the beans by 3 inches. With the lid on, bring the beans to a boil, then reduce the heat to medium. Simmer the

beans for 1 hour, stirring occasionally and making sure the beans remain submerged under at least 2 inches of water. You may need to add 2 cups of water every 20 minutes to make sure the beans stay submerged.

4. After 1 hour, remove the lid and increase the heat to high. Cook until half of the beans have broken their skin and the bean starches have turned the water murky, about 30 minutes. You will need to add water during this process. If none of the beans have broken their skin, boil on high for an additional 30 minutes, stirring occasionally and making sure the beans are always submerged under 2 inches of water.

5. After about half of the beans break their skin, continue boiling and allow the water level to go down to the same level as the beans. You should be able to easily smash the beans between your fingers. At this point, decide whether to make coarse or smooth red bean paste.

6. For tsubu-an (coarse) bean paste, thoroughly mash half of the beans with a potato masher. Do not add additional water. Return the mashed beans to the pot.

7. For koshi-an (smooth) bean paste, transfer all of the beans to a blender or food processor, purée them, and return them to the pot.

8. Add the sugar to the bean paste and cook over medium heat for 10 minutes, then turn off the heat. The beans should start to look darker and shinier. Let the beans cool to room temperature, then refrigerate for at least 1 hour. Your bean paste is now ready to use! Bean paste can easily be refrigerated for 1 week in an airtight container or frozen for up to 2 weeks.

TRADITIONAL SHIRO-AN
(SWEET WHITE BEAN PASTE)

Sweet white bean paste has a lighter, more refined flavor than sweet red bean paste. For this reason, you can easily flavor white bean paste with any kind of extracts or flavorings. Making shiro-an does take some time and labor, so it is best done with friends. Fortunately, the paste can be easily frozen and saved for future mochi fillings. This recipe holds a special memory for me — Haruko Nagaishi, a third-generation Japanese-American woman living in the Bay Area, taught me how to make this delicious paste. Haruko-san's recipe is adapted from the San Jose Wesley Methodist Church cookbook. You'll need a food processor or blender; and a dish towel, muslin cloth, or white cotton cloth with a tight weave. You will need to soak the beans overnight, so plan ahead.

NOTE: By replacing the large lima beans with baby lima beans, you can prepare the recipe more quickly, since you won't have to remove the skin from the small beans. Either way, you end up with a very smooth paste.

INGREDIENTS

- 1 **pound dried large or baby lima beans (see note)**
- 5 **cups boiling water**
- 2 **cups sugar**
- **Pinch of salt**

YIELD:
ABOUT
2½ CUPS
(FOR
30 BALLS)

DIRECTIONS

1. The day before you plan to make the paste, place the beans in a large heatproof bowl and pour in enough of the boiling water to cover the beans by 2 inches. Let the beans soak overnight.

2. The next day, drain the beans and remove all the skins and sprouts. This must be done with your hands, one bean at a time. This is best done with a friend, as it can take up to an hour on your own. Skip the skinning if you are using baby lima beans.

3. Transfer the beans to a large pot, and add enough water to cover the beans by 2 inches. Bring to a boil, then drain. Repeat this two more times. (This removes the scum, the bean's gas-inducing properties, and the strong bean flavor.)

4. Add enough water to cover the beans by 1 inch, bring to a boil, then reduce the heat and simmer until the beans are soft, fork-tender, and easy to smash between your fingers, 30 to 60 minutes. This is a large range in cooking time, but recently harvested dried beans will cook faster than older dried beans. If the water level goes down, replenish so that it remains 1 inch above the beans.

5. Transfer the beans and water to a food processor or blender, and purée until very smooth. Lay a dish towel over a fine-mesh strainer, then pour the purée into the

Recipe continues on next page

towel. Grab and twist the towel to wring out excess liquid from the purée. Wring vigorously to remove all the water. Open the towel and make an indentation in the paste with your finger. If the indentation stays, then you're done wringing. The paste should be the texture of mashed potatoes.

6. Transfer the beans to a large pot, stir in the sugar and salt, and simmer over low heat, stirring occasionally, until a solid mixture is formed, 15 to 20 minutes.

7. Cool and form into balls about 1 inch in diameter. Store in the fridge for up to 4 days or in the freezer for up to 1 month.

VARIATION: Add 1 teaspoon matcha to every cup of prepared sweet white bean paste for a matcha-flavored white bean paste.

STRAWBERRY MOCHI, TWO WAYS

WHOLE STRAWBERRIES

STRAWBERRIES AND BEAN PASTE are a popular combination and are frequently used as filling in mochi. You can leave the strawberry whole or slice it. If whole, cut off the leafy hull, then cover the strawberry with 1 tablespoon of red or white bean paste, leaving the cut part free of paste (see photo on page 27). Working carefully, place the tip of the strawberry on top of a flattened piece of mochi and wrap the mochi up around the strawberry, pinching to seal over the cut end of the strawberry.

SLICED STRAWBERRIES

SLICED STRAWBERRIES are easier to use as filling and are very pretty. Cut off the leafy hulls, then horizontally slice the strawberries into circles about ½ inch wide. Place a strawberry disk on a piece of mochi. Set a 1-inch ball of red or white bean paste on top of the strawberry disk, and push down slightly to flatten the ball into a disk shape, similar to the strawberry (as shown below). Pinch the mochi over top of the red bean paste to seal. Enjoy!

MODERN FILLINGS

VANILLA CUSTARD FILLING

INGREDIENTS

- 1 cup plus 2 tablespoons whole milk
- 2½ tablespoons cornstarch
- 2 large egg yolks
- 4 tablespoons sugar
- 1 teaspoon pure vanilla extract
- 1 tablespoon unsalted butter

YIELD:
8-10
PIECES

This tasty, simple-to-make filling can be used with various flavors of mochi. The custard sets up firm, making it easy to pinch the mochi around it, but it softens with the heat from warm mochi. Puddinglike in texture, rich and creamy with a slight taste of vanilla, it is delicious! This custard recipe was created with love by my friend Eri Combs of Eri's Bakery (erisbakery.com). It pairs well with Matcha Mochi (page 39), Chocolate Mochi (page 41), Steamed White Daifuku Mochi (page 28), or Rosewater Mochi (page 46).

DIRECTIONS

1. Warm the 1 cup milk in a medium saucepan over medium-high heat until it starts to simmer, whisking occasionally to prevent burning.

2. While the milk is heating, whisk together the cornstarch and the 2 tablespoons milk in a medium bowl, making sure the cornstarch is fully dissolved. Add the egg yolks and sugar, and whisk until thoroughly combined.

3. When the milk starts to simmer, take it off the heat. Gradually add 2 tablespoons of hot milk at a time to the yolk mixture, whisking while doing so, until half of the milk is combined with the eggs. Then add the other half and whisk. Once the milk is fully incorporated, scrape

the mixture back into the pan. Whisking constantly, heat the custard until bubbling. Continue whisking for 2 minutes longer. When the custard looks smooth and glossy, take the pan off the heat.

4. Whisk in the vanilla, followed by the butter. Mix until everything is incorporated (if you see any lumps, put the mixture through a strainer). Transfer the custard to a container and lay a piece of plastic wrap directly on the surface. Let the custard cool in the refrigerator for 1 to 2 hours.

5. Cut the cooled custard into 1-inch squares and use inside your mochi.

VARIATIONS: *To make* **Matcha Custard**, *reduce the vanilla to ½ teaspoon and add 1 teaspoon sifted matcha to the cornstarch.*

Instead of vanilla, add 1 teaspoon of other extracts, such as lemon or almond, to vary the flavor of your custard. Mix in the extract in step 4, when you add the butter.

HAUPIA PUDDING

Haupia is a traditional coconut pudding eaten in Hawaii. The haupia pudding filling in this recipe is light and creamy, not heavy, and the uplifting flavor of coconut pervades this dish. Use it to fill the Coconut Mochi dough (page 48). You'll need an eight-inch square pan.

INGREDIENTS

- **1 cup coconut milk**
- **¾ cup water**
- **⅓ cup sugar**
- **¼ cup cornstarch**
- **Pinch of salt**

DIRECTIONS

1. Whisk together the coconut milk, water, sugar, corn-starch and salt in a medium saucepan until thoroughly uniform in texture.

2. Set the pot over medium heat. Whisking constantly, cook until the mixture comes to a boil and thickens.

3. Pour the pudding into an 8-inch square pan (or other small pan), cover with plastic wrap or a lid, and refrigerate until firm, about 3 hours.

4. Once firm, the pudding can be cut into 16 squares, or however many squares you would like for the filling.

YIELD:
16
PIECES

MATCHA MOCHI (page 39) with
MATCHA CREAM CHEESE FILLING

MATCHA CREAM CHEESE FILLING

Creamy, light, with the flavor of matcha, this mochi filling is so delicious that your friends and family will beg you to make more every time they see you! And you'll say yes, because it's also easy to create and assemble.

INGREDIENTS

- ¾ cup confectioners' sugar
- 2 teaspoons matcha, plus more as needed
- 1 (8-ounce) package full-fat cream cheese

DIRECTIONS

1. Sift together the sugar and matcha.

2. Place the cream cheese in a microwavable bowl. Microwave on high for 15 seconds to soften. (Alternatively, let the cream cheese sit on the counter at room temperature until it has softened.) Beat the softened cheese with a spatula until smooth.

3. Stir the matcha mixture into the cream cheese until completely incorporated and uniform in color. If lumps of matcha remain, you may need to use a hand mixer. Taste and add more matcha as needed. Some brands have a lighter flavor than others.

4. Refrigerate the mixture for 1 hour.

5. Using a spoon and wet hands, make balls 1½ inches in diameter. Place these on a sheet of parchment paper in an airtight container in the fridge for at least 1 hour to solidify. Do not freeze the cream cheese balls, as the texture may change. This mixture can be kept in the refrigerator for up to 4 days.

YIELD:
12
BALLS

BLACK SESAME CREAM CHEESE FILLING

This creamy black sesame paste made with cream cheese and freshly ground roasted black sesame seeds, with hints of honey and kinako, is a great filling for Steamed White Daifuku Mochi (page 28). The kinako powder is optional but adds delicious flavor.

INGREDIENTS

- 1 (8-ounce) package full-fat cream cheese
- 2½ tablespoons roasted black sesame seeds (see note)
- ½ cup confectioners' sugar
- 1 tablespoon honey
- 1 teaspoon kinako (optional)

DIRECTIONS

1. If the cream cheese has been in the fridge, let it come to room temperature. Alternatively, microwave it on high for 15 seconds to soften.

2. Grind the seeds in a spice grinder or mortar and pestle until the seeds turn into a fine powder.

3. Thoroughly combine the seeds with the cream cheese in a medium bowl. Add the sugar, honey, and kinako, and mix until the mixture has an even consistency. It should be dark gray and speckled.

4. Lay a piece of parchment paper on a plate or baking sheet. Using a spoon and wet hands, make 12 balls that are each 1½ inches wide. Refrigerate for 1 hour, or overnight. Remove from the refrigerator right before use. This mixture can be kept in the refrigerator for up to 4 days.

YIELD:
10
BALLS

NOTE: If you can't find roasted black sesame seeds, simply heat raw sesame seeds in a dry pan over medium heat, stirring until the seeds begin to smoke slightly, then turn the heat off. The seeds are ready to use right away.

STEAMED WHITE DAIFUKU MOCHI (page 28) with
BLACK SESAME CREAM CHEESE FILLING

ROSEWATER MOCHI (page 46) with
STRAWBERRY–CREAM CHEESE FILLING

STRAWBERRY-ROSE CREAM CHEESE FILLING

This creamy strawberry filling has a slight hint of rose. Omit the rose water if you do not like it, but it will enhance the strawberry flavor. This filling is delicious inside Steamed White Daifuku Mochi (page 28) or Rosewater Mochi (page 46).

INGREDIENTS

- 1 (8-ounce) package full-fat cream cheese
- 2 tablespoons strawberry jam
- ¼ cup confectioners' sugar
- 1 teaspoon rose water, such as Cortas brand

DIRECTIONS

1. If the cream cheese has been in the fridge, let it sit for 30 minutes at room temperature. Alternatively, microwave it on high for 15 seconds to soften.

2. Combine the cream cheese, jam, sugar, and rose water in a medium bowl. Mix with a spatula until thoroughly combined.

3. Using a spoon and wet hands, make 12 balls that are each 1½ inches wide. Place, evenly spaced, on a parchment paper–lined plate or baking sheet.

4. Refrigerate for at least 1 hour. Remove from the refrigerator right before use. This mixture can be kept in the refrigerator for up to 4 days.

VARIATION: *For a rich and creamy* **Oreo Cream Cheese Filling**, *replace the jam and rose water with 10 chocolate sandwich cookies, crushed fine (including the sandwich filling) in a mortar and pestle. Use it to fill white daifuku mochi (pages 28 and 35) or Chocolate Mochi (page 41).*

YIELD:
10
BALLS

TARO PASTE FILLING

This taro filling is simple to make and features the natural taro flavor with a hint of coconut. It's perfect for putting inside mochi! I prefer the large taro variety (dark brown color), but any type of taro can be used. You'll need a food processor or blender for this recipe, which can be easily doubled or tripled.

INGREDIENTS

5 **cups water**

1 **large taro, peeled and roughly chopped into ½-inch cubes (about 3 cups)**

⅔ **cup sugar**

½ **cup coconut milk**

YIELD:
15-20
BALLS

DIRECTIONS

1. Bring the water to a boil in a large pan. Add the taro and cook over medium heat, stirring occasionally, until fork-tender, 10 to 20 minutes. Do not overcook or the taro may get too mushy and the final texture may not be as good. Drain and cool the taro for 10 minutes. Chop off and discard any parts that may have turned brown during cooking.

2. Combine the taro, sugar, and coconut milk in a food processor or blender. Blend until smooth and even in consistency.

3. Transfer the mixture to a shallow, microwavable dish (such as a glass pie pan). Microwave on high for 3 minutes, then stir the mixture with a spatula. Microwave for another 2 minutes, and stir. If the mixture still looks like a liquid, stir it and then microwave it for 2 minutes longer. The mixture should now look more like a paste instead of a liquid. As it cools, it will become firmer.

4. Cool to room temperature, then place in an airtight container. To prevent a crust forming on the paste, put plastic wrap directly on top of the paste. The paste can be used at room temperature, but it is easier to handle once it has cooled in the fridge for at least 1 hour. Store in the refrigerator for 3 days or the freezer for up to a month. To make it easier to fill mochi, use a 2-inch scoop to shape the taro paste into balls and let them harden in the freezer.

CHOCOLATE AND PEANUT BUTTER FILLING

This recipe was inspired by the mind-bogglingly delicious mochi at Maui Specialty Chocolates in Maui, Hawaii. I clearly remember taking my first bite of a mochi with this filling and being instantly transformed into a peanut butter mochi lover. I am not usually a peanut butter fan, but somehow the combination of gooey chocolate and chunky peanut butter with the chewy bite of white mochi is so satisfying. This filling pairs well with Microwaved White Daifuku Mochi (page 35) or Chocolate Mochi (page 41). Bring this to your next event and you will be the talk of the party!

INGREDIENTS

- ½ cup milk chocolate chips
- 1 cup chunky or smooth peanut butter

DIRECTIONS

1. Pour the chocolate chips into a microwavable bowl, and microwave on high heat for 30 seconds at a time, stirring well after each heating, until completely melted. Add the peanut butter and stir well until fully incorporated. Refrigerate for 2 hours to cool.

2. Using a spoon or small ice cream scoop, scoop out 10 equal-sized balls of filling. Use the filling right away, or place the balls in an airtight container and refrigerate for up to 1 week.

PB AND JAM

For a classic peanut butter and strawberry jam filling, spoon 2 teaspoons of jam into one mold of an ice cube tray, then spoon 2 teaspoons of peanut butter on top of the jam. Repeat to fill nine more molds (you don't need to fill the entire tray). Freeze for 1 hour, or overnight. Remove the ice cube tray from the freezer right before filling your mochi, and use a spoon to pop out the fillings!

YIELD:
10
BALLS

TRUFFLE FILLINGS

CHOCOLATE TRUFFLE FILLING

Smooth and decadent, this truffle is the perfect pairing for Chocolate Mochi (page 41). It was inspired by the delicious dark chocolate mochi made by Maui Specialty Chocolates in Maui, Hawaii. The soft and chewy outer mochi with the light yet dense chocolate on the inside is a match made in heaven.

INGREDIENTS

- 1 cup semisweet chocolate chips
- ½ cup heavy cream
- 1 tablespoon unsalted butter
- ⅛ teaspoon salt
- ½ cup unsweetened cocoa powder, for coating (optional)

DIRECTIONS

1. Combine the chocolate chips, cream, butter, and salt in a medium microwavable bowl. Microwave on high for 30 seconds, then mix with a fork or small whisk. The butter and chips should start melting at this point.

2. Microwave for another 30 seconds. Whisk until the chocolate is completely dissolved and incorporated and the mixture is smooth, with no lumps. If the chocolate is not fully dissolved, heat the mixture again in the microwave in 15-second increments, whisking after each, until fully dissolved.

3. Cool the chocolate mixture to room temperature, then cover with plastic wrap and refrigerate until slightly firm to the touch, about 30 minutes.

YIELD:
8-10 BALLS

4. Using a spoon, scoop out a rounded 1½-inch ball of truffle mixture. Repeat to make 10 balls. Coat each piece with cocoa powder, if using, and shape it into a ball with your hands. Place on a parchment sheet in an airtight container in the refrigerator for at least 1 hour. Remove from the refrigerator right before use. The filling can be refrigerated for up to 1 week or frozen for up to 1 month.

GOOEY OR DENSE?

If eaten when your mochi is freshly made and hot, these truffles can be warm and gooey, like chocolate lava cake. Or they can be soft yet dense if left to cool at room temperature. Either way, mochi filled with truffles are fantastic!

MATCHA TRUFFLE FILLING

This is one addictive mochi truffle, loaded with good-quality white chocolate, matcha, and cream. This truffle pairs excellently with Matcha Mochi (page 39) and when eaten hot, delicious matcha goodness drips out with one bite, like a matcha lava cake. If eaten at room temperature, the truffle will have a chewy texture.

INGREDIENTS

- 1 cup (170 g) good-quality white chocolate chips, such as Ghirardelli
- 5 tablespoons unsalted butter, chopped
- 3 tablespoons heavy cream
- 1½ teaspoons matcha, sifted
- Confectioners' sugar, for dusting (optional)

DIRECTIONS

1. Combine the chocolate chips, butter, and cream in a medium microwavable bowl. Microwave on high in 30-second increments, stirring well after each, until melted, about 1½ minutes total. White chocolate can overheat easily, so it's best to stop heating it before all the chips are melted; stir with a fork or small whisk until the remaining heat melts all the chocolate. Once the mixture is smooth, add the matcha and whisk again until evenly incorporated.

2. Cover the bowl with plastic wrap. Let cool to room temperature for 30 minutes, then refrigerate until the mixture is firm to the touch, 1½ hours.

3. Using a small spoon, scoop out 15 equal-sized pieces of the truffle mixture. Dust your hands with powdered sugar to prevent stickiness, if desired, and round each piece into a 1½-inch ball. Place the balls on a parchment paper sheet in an airtight container in the refrigerator for at least 1 hour, or overnight. Remove from the refrigerator right before use. The balls can be stored in the refrigerator for up to 1 week or in the freezer for up to 1 month.

YIELD:
15
BALLS

VARIATION: For **Black Sesame Truffle Filling**, omit the matcha and instead add 2 tablespoons of ground roasted black sesame seeds. You can finely grind the sesame seeds in a spice grinder or in a mortar and pestle.

TIPS FOR CREATING YOUR OWN FILLINGS

How do you create your own unique mochi flavor combination? I often first look at classic flavor combinations that work well together in other dishes. But don't be afraid to experiment and pull inspiration from many cultures and cuisines.

Consider the desserts you already love — if you're like me, you may love the taste of sponge cake topped with homemade whipped cream and fresh strawberries. Or if you're like my husband, you may love chocolate in everything!

What are your favorite flavor combinations? Because mochi can easily be flavored on the inside *and* outside, you can most likely find a way to incorporate your favorite flavor combos into your mochi creations. I hope this section serves as a starting platform for you to experiment with your own unique flavors.

EARL GREY TRUFFLE FILLING

This truffle is rich with high-quality white chocolate, and you can definitely taste the Earl Grey tea. Eating this smooth and chewy fragrant truffle is a memorable experience.
It pairs well with Microwaved White Daifuku Mochi (page 35).

INGREDIENTS

4 tablespoons heavy cream

2 bags Earl Grey tea, tags and metal staples removed (I use Trader Joe's organic tea)

1 cup (170 g) good-quality white chocolate chips (Ghirardelli is best)

5 tablespoons unsalted butter, chopped

Confectioner's sugar, for dusting (optional)

DIRECTIONS

1. Pour the cream into a medium microwavable bowl. Add the tea bags, making sure to submerge the bags in the cream. Microwave on high for 30 seconds. Stir the mixture a few times to help the tea seep into the cream, being careful not to tear the tea bags while doing this. (It is preferable that no tea leaves get into the mixture.)

2. Microwave for another 15 seconds, and press the tea bags with a fork. Remove and discard the tea bags. The cream should be light brown at this point.

3. Add the chocolate chips and butter to the infused cream. Microwave in 30-second increments, stirring after each, or until the chocolate and butter are melted, about 1½ minutes total. Stir with a fork until the remaining heat melts all the chocolate. The mixture may look grainy initially, but as you continue to stir it should smooth out.

4. Cover the bowl with plastic wrap. Refrigerate until the mixture is firm to the touch, 1 to 1½ hours.

5. Using a small spoon, scoop out 15 equal-sized pieces of the truffle mixture. Dust your hands with powdered sugar to prevent stickiness, if desired, and round each piece into a 1½-inch ball. Place the balls on a parchment paper sheet in an airtight container in the refrigerator for at least 1 hour, or overnight. Remove from the refrigerator right before use. Store the balls in the refrigerator for up to 1 week or in the freezer for up to 1 month.

YIELD:
15
BALLS

FRESH FRUIT FILLING IDEAS

Peanut Butter and Banana: ½-inch-thick slice of banana topped with 1 rounded teaspoon of peanut butter

Peach with Bean Paste: ½-inch-thick disk of peach topped with 1 rounded teaspoon of red bean or white bean paste

Kiwifruit and Bean Paste: ½-inch-thick disk of kiwifruit topped with 1 rounded teaspoon of red bean or white bean paste

Blueberry and Bean Paste: 3 blueberries topped with 1 rounded teaspoon of red bean or white bean paste

Grape with Bean Paste: 1 whole grape covered entirely by a thin layer of red bean or white bean paste

Raspberry with Chocolate Truffle: 1 raspberry and 1 chocolate truffle (page 76)

Strawberry with Strawberry-Rose Truffle: ½-inch-thick disk of strawberry and 1 strawberry-rose truffle (page 82)

Chocolate Banana: ½-inch-thick slice of banana and 1 chocolate truffle

Chocolate Strawberry: ½-inch-thick disk of strawberry and 1 chocolate truffle

Strawberry and Matcha Truffle: ½-inch-thick disk of strawberry and 1 matcha truffle (page 78).

STRAWBERRY-ROSE TRUFFLE FILLING

This filling features freeze-dried strawberries, which can be easily bought at any grocery store. The strawberries are pulverized and combined with rose water and melted white chocolate. The resulting truffles are creamy, with the essence of strawberry in them! You'll need a clean spice grinder for this recipe. This truffle pairs well with white daifuku mochi (page 28 or 35) and especially well with Rosewater Mochi (page 46).

INGREDIENTS

- ⅓ cup freeze-dried strawberries
- 1 cup (170 g) good-quality white chocolate chips, such as Ghirardelli
- 5 tablespoons unsalted butter, chopped
- 3 tablespoons heavy cream
- ½ teaspoon rose water, such as Cortas brand
- Confectioners' sugar, for dusting (optional)

YIELD:
15
BALLS

DIRECTIONS

1. Spoon the strawberries into a spice grinder or mortar and pestle and grind to a fine powder.

2. Combine the chocolate chips, butter, and cream in a medium microwavable bowl. Microwave on high in 30-second increments, stirring after each, until melted, about 1½ minutes total. White chocolate can overheat easily, so it's best to stop heating it before all the chips are melted; stir with a fork or small whisk until the remaining heat melts all the chocolate. Once the mixture is smooth, add the strawberry powder and whisk again until everything is evenly incorporated. Whisk in the rose water until incorporated.

3. Cover the bowl with plastic wrap. Refrigerate until the mixture is firm to the touch, 1½ hours.

4. Using a small spoon, scoop out 15 equal pieces of the truffle mixture. Dust your hands with powdered sugar to prevent stickiness, if desired, and round each piece into a 1½-inch ball. Place the balls on a parchment paper sheet in an airtight container in the refrigerator for at least 1 hour, or overnight. Remove from the refrigerator right before use. Store in the refrigerator for up to 1 week or in the freezer for up to 1 month.

FRUIT JUICE- OR EXTRACT-INFUSED BEAN PASTE

To add a fruit flavor to your mochi, I highly recommend placing a piece of fresh fruit inside the mochi. But if nothing fresh is on hand, you could add fruit juice or extract to the bean paste. Possibilities include juice from passion fruit, mango, pear, guava, and pineapple. Simply mix together the bean paste and juice or extract in a microwavable bowl and heat for the amount of time specified below. Allow the infused bean paste to cool in the refrigerator until firm before using, at least 1 hour. The recipes below can easily be doubled and tripled.

BEAN PASTE	FRUIT JUICE/EXTRACT	MICROWAVE TIME
½ cup	3 tablespoons juice OR ½ teaspoon extract	2 minutes
1 cup	6 tablespoons juice OR 1 teaspoon extract	3½ minutes

MOCHI ICE CREAM

People all over the world love mochi ice cream. This treat debuted in 1981, when the company Lotte began selling Yukimi Daifuku, but it wasn't until 1994 that Frances Hashimoto came up with the current version of mochi ice cream sold in the United States. Many people are surprised to learn that mochi ice cream is easy to make at home. The main trick for using it in mochi is to scoop the ice cream into small balls and freeze them in advance. Otherwise, you'll have a mess of rapidly melting ice cream when you envelope it with warm mochi. You can certainly use homemade ice cream to fill your mochi (and we encourage you to do so if you have the time!), but we use good-quality store-bought ice cream for ease and efficiency.

MOCHI ICE CREAM

INGREDIENTS

1 **pint ice cream of your choice**

1 **batch Microwaved White Daifuku Mochi (page 35)**

Cornstarch

DIRECTIONS

1. Scoop the ice cream into seven 2-inch-wide balls, and place each ball in a cupcake liner in an airtight container. Freeze for at least 2 hours, or overnight.

2. After the ice cream has been frozen for at least 2 hours, prepare the mochi dough through step 6 of the directions on page 35, dusting the board with at least ⅓ cup of cornstarch. Be sure to use a large cutting board, since this mochi dough will be rolled flat and will need ample space.

3. Generously dust the top of the mochi dough and a rolling pin with cornstarch. Push down on the mochi to flatten it, then roll it to ¼-inch thickness.

4. Using a 4-inch circular cookie cutter, cut out seven 4-inch circles of dough.

YIELD:
7
PIECES

Recipe continues on page 88

MOCHI + ICE CREAM PAIRING IDEAS

- **Rosewater Mochi** (page 46) with strawberry ice cream
- **Matcha Mochi** (page 39) with matcha ice cream
- **Chocolate Mochi** (page 41) with matcha ice cream
- **Matcha Mochi** with strawberry ice cream
- **Mango Mochi** (page 50) with mango ice cream
- **Chocolate Mochi** with chocolate ice cream
- **Chocolate Mochi** with coffee ice cream
- **Chocolate Mochi** with salted caramel ice cream

5. Working with one circle at a time, remove a ball of ice cream from the freezer, remove the cupcake liner, and place the ball upside down in the center of the circle. Pull up the dough corners and pinch to seal the seams around the ice cream. Place the mochi seam side down on a fresh cupcake liner, then freeze. The ice cream will start melting almost immediately, so it's important to assemble and freeze each mochi quickly and individually.

6. Once all the mochi ice creams are assembled, freeze them for at least 1 hour. To enjoy the mochi ice cream, let it soften at room temperature for 2 minutes before eating.

DECORATING MOCHI

Decorating mochi is a great activity for people of all ages — including young children — if you have the right tools. Edible markers, chocolate chips, and candy eyes are ideal when kids decorate mochi.

Decorating can be easy or time consuming. If you use the supplies and techniques described on pages 92 and 94, it is fairly easy and quick to decorate your mochi. If you have time for a little project, try making some cute mochi flowers or animals with *nerikiri*, a mixture of sweet white bean paste and mochi dough used in traditional Japanese *wagashi* (sweet treats). Because it is pliable, nerikiri dough is perfect for forming decorations to top your mochi. I use nerikiri dough to decorate any kind of filled daifuku mochi, such as white mochi filled with red bean paste.

EASY DECORATING MATERIALS AND TIPS

Edible-ink markers. Looking for the easiest way to decorate your mochi? I highly recommend edible-ink markers, which you can buy at craft stores or online. They come in different colors and can be used to draw designs directly on the mochi. Guests in our classes have lots of fun getting creative and drawing with markers. Make sure to brush the starch off the top of the mochi before drawing on it so that it draws clearly and doesn't get stuck on the starch.

Candy eyes. Easily bought from any craft store, candy eyes immediately bring cuteness and character to your mochi. Stick two eyes on your mochi and draw some hair, or stick on several eyes and make a cute monster! You can get very creative with candy eyes.

Chocolate chips. Chocolate chips can serve as eyes and mouths for your mochi. For a mouth, place one chip in the mouth region for a cute, surprised look. Or melt ½ cup of chocolate chips in a glass or ceramic bowl in the microwave, stirring after each 10-second heating incre-ment, until the chips are fully melted. Carefully spoon or pour the chocolate into a small plastic frosting bag, then let cool for a few minutes. When the chocolate is thicker and less runny, snip off a tiny corner of the bag. Use the chocolate to draw on eyes, a mouth, or whatever features you would like.

Sprinkles. These, too, can be used for eyes or different features on your mochi. For greater drama, paint the top of your mochi with water, then dip the moistened area into a bowl of sprinkles so the sprinkles adhere and completely coat the top. Or dip the entire mochi in water, shake off the excess, and roll the mochi in the sprinkles, fully covering the mochi with these tiny candies for a party-worthy, festive look.

Edible shimmer powder. You can find this at any craft or cake store. First, brush the excess starch off the mochi. Then dip a brush into the shimmer powder and paint directly onto the dry mochi. Your mochi will look like an iridescent pearl (a tasty one at that!).

Kinako or peanut powder, black sesame seeds, and coconut flakes. Coating the outside of your mochi with powder, black sesame seeds, or coconut gives it a beautiful, natural look. Kinako and peanut powder can be bought at your local Asian store or online, as can black sesame seeds. You can also make the powders. Dip your mochi in water, shake off the excess, and drop it into a bowl with coconut flakes or an edible powder of your choice. Roll the mochi around until it is fully coated. Then it's ready to enjoy! You can even grind up cookies, such as Oreos, and use them as a coating!

MOCHI PARTY CHECKLIST

Mochi-making parties are a fun way to spend time with friends while creating something delicious. I suggest you prepare the Microwaved White Daifuku Mochi (page 35), Rosewater Mochi (page 46), and/or Matcha Mochi (page 39), and triple the recipe for a party. And after you're done making and filling each mochi, get your creative juices flowing and decorate them!

Materials

- ☐ Disposable plastic tablecloth, to cover table
- ☐ 10 cupcake liners per guest
- ☐ Pastry brushes
- ☐ Plates for fresh fruit
- ☐ Large cutting board for the person distributing the mochi
- ☐ Large mixing bowls
- ☐ Large ceramic or glass microwavable bowls
- ☐ Whisks
- ☐ Edible markers
- ☐ Containers for guests to take mochi home

Ingredients

- ☐ Fresh-cut strawberries and other fresh fruits as desired (such as blueberries, raspberries, mango, and kiwifruit)
- ☐ Cornstarch (at least 2 pounds)
- ☐ Mochiko (3 pounds will make about 70 mochi pieces)
- ☐ Granulated sugar (5 cups will be enough for 3 boxes of mochiko)
- ☐ Chocolate chips (white, chocolate, colored; feel free to buy unique flavors, too!)
- ☐ 5 cups sweet red bean paste (home-made, or in a pinch, this can be bought at an Asian grocery store)
- ☐ Matcha (optional for making matcha mochi)
- ☐ Rose water and a red food coloring or natural beet powder to make the mochi a pink color (optional)

AUTHENTIC NERIKIRI DOUGH

This nerikiri dough is very easy to make once you have sweet white bean paste. It has the texture of playdough, so it is perfect for dyeing with colors and using for decorating your filled daifuku mochi — especially for making cute faces.

Nerikiri dough can be tightly sealed and frozen for up to a month. It can be easily reheated until it is pliable again, and ready to use. You can make the dough ahead of time and freeze it for up to 1 month or refrigerate for up to 4 days.

INGREDIENTS

- ¼ cup mochiko
- ¼ cup water
- 1 cup freshly made sweet white bean paste (page 58)
- Food coloring of choice

TIP: If you don't have time to mix up nerikiri, roll and cut out thin sheets of colored mochi dough.

DIRECTIONS

1. Combine the mochiko and water in a small microwavable bowl, stirring until smooth. Microwave on high for 45 seconds, mix thoroughly again, then let this mochi dough cool for 2 minutes.

2. Combine the mochi dough and the bean paste, and knead them together with your hands until the dough is a uniform texture, 1 to 2 minutes. Add food coloring, if using (see box on facing page). Chill in the refrigerator until ready to use. If the final dough is too wet, add 1 tablespoon of mochiko flour at a time until it is the texture of playdough. It should not stick to your fingers too much.

3. To use, roll out the nerikiri dough into a thin layer and use it to cover your already filled daifuku mochi. Add eyes, a mouth, and other features to make a cute face (see pages 102 to 105).

YIELD:
1
CUP

HOW TO COLOR NERIKIRI DOUGH

Form ⅓ cup of nerikiri dough into a smooth ball with your hands. Squeeze 1 drop of liquid food coloring onto the ball, then knead by hand until the dough is uniform in color (you may want to use gloves for this to prevent staining your hands). Round the dough into a smooth ball, wrap in plastic wrap, and set it aside. If it starts sticking to your hands, dust your hands with a pinch of mochiko.

QUICK AND EASY NERIKIRI DOUGH

This nerikiri dough relies on canned beans, so you can skip the step of making fresh sweet white bean paste from scratch. This is a good option to use if you are in a time crunch. For a fresher taste, follow the Authentic Nerikiri Dough recipe on page 96.

INGREDIENTS

- 2 (15.5-ounce) cans cannellini beans, rinsed and drained
- 4 cups boiling water, or more as needed
- ½ cup sugar
- ¼ cup mochiko
- ¼ cup cold water, plus more as needed

DIRECTIONS

1. Place the beans in a large heatproof bowl. Pour in enough of the boiling water to cover the beans by 1 inch. Soak the beans for 10 minutes, then transfer to a fine-mesh strainer to drain. Rinse the beans under cold running water. (Soaking and rinsing remove some of the beany smell and taste.)

2. Set the strainer atop a medium microwavable bowl. Using a spatula or rice spoon, press the beans against the walls of the strainer to separate the skins from the bean paste. Continue to smash and push the beans against the strainer in a side-to-side motion until you've pressed all the beans through the mesh. A lot of skins will be left behind; these can be discarded. Stir sugar into the bean paste.

3. Microwave the bean paste for 2 minutes, stir, and then microwave for 1 minute longer. Stir and let cool. At this point, you should be able to make a lasting indentation in the bean paste with your finger and the paste should not stick to your fingers. If it sticks, microwave for 1 minute longer. Alternatively, if the paste cracks, it is too dry. In that case, add 1 teaspoon of water and stir until a thick but smooth paste forms. You should have about 1 cup of bean paste. Set aside.

4. In a separate bowl, mix together the mochiko and the cold water in a small microwavable bowl until smooth. Microwave on high for 45 seconds, then let this mochi dough cool for 2 minutes.

YIELD:
1½ CUPS

5. Add the bean paste to the mochi dough and mix together with a spoon until uniform in texture. Squish the dough together with your hands for about 2 minutes until the mixture is soft and pliable. If you see pieces of white mochi, continue to knead the dough until it is a uniform color. Add food coloring, if using (see box on page 97). Wrap in plastic to prevent drying, and chill in the refrigerator until ready to use. It will keep in the refrigerator for up to 4 days or in the freezer for up to 1 month.

6. To use, roll out the nerikiri dough into a thin layer and use it to cover your already filled daifuku mochi. Add eyes, a mouth, and other features to make a cute face (see pages 102 to 105).

EASY PINK MOCHI FLOWERS

These great decorations really boost your mochi presentation. You'll need a Russian piping tip or a cookie cutter that cuts 1-inch-diameter circles.

1. Roll Rosewater Mochi (page 46) to ¼-inch thickness.

2. Using a Russian piping tip or a 1-inch circular cookie cutter, cut the dough into circles.

3. Starting from the top, layer 8 petals on top of each other. Then, roll tightly from the bottom to the top.

4. Cut the rolled dough in half to make 2 flowers.

BABY CHICK MOCHI

A cute yellow chick brings brightness in springtime!

Two (¾-inch-long) rods of nerikiri dough, pressed flat to form the head feathers

Two (1-inch-long) rods of nerikiri dough to form the wings

1. Make and fill your daifuku mochi.

2. Roll yellow nerikiri dough to ¼-inch thickness and cover the mochi with it. At this point, you can add the other facial features using different colors of nerikiri dough.

PANDA BEAR MOCHI

Here is a panda bear mochi that is almost too cute to eat.
Bean paste works best to create the ideal mochi shape for animals;
filling with fresh fruit can make the mochi lopsided.

············· ½-inch-wide
black candy
pearls

1. Make and fill your daifuku mochi.

2. Roll white nerikiri dough to ¼-inch thickness and cover the
mochi with it. At this point, you can add the other facial features
using black nerikiri dough.

BABY BEAR MOCHI

This adorable brown-and-white bear is deliciously edible.

1. Make and fill your daifuku mochi.

2. Roll brown nerikiri dough to ¼-inch thickness and cover the mochi with it. At this point, you can add the other facial features using more nerikiri dough.

PIG MOCHI

This little piggy will bring pep to your beautiful mochi!

1. Make and fill your daifuku mochi.

2. Roll pink nerikiri dough to ¼-inch thickness and cover the mochi with it. At this point, you can add the other facial features using more nerikiri dough.

A New Year's Tradition: POUNDED MOCHI

Pounded mochi is the most traditional form of Japanese mochi. In its essence, pounded mochi requires only Japanese sweet rice and water. This mochi is amazingly chewy and stretchy and is pleasing to the eye (think of stretching mozzarella cheese). Pounded mochi is denser and chewier than dessert mochi, which is made with mochi rice flour.

POUNDED MOCHI Q & A

Q: Can I store pounded mochi after making it?

A: Yes, you can easily freeze pounded mochi. Once it has cooled to room temperature, simply transfer it to a freezer-safe container, then store in the freezer for up to 2 months. Reheat the mochi for soup, or toast it, as needed. After cooling, do not leave pounded mochi out at room temperature, or it will quickly go bad.

Q: Is eating pounded mochi safe for all ages?

A: Pounded mochi should be eaten with caution, as it can be very sticky and dense. If you eat pounded mochi in large bites or you don't chew it well, it can catch in your throat. This is a concern especially for older folks and young children. Please be sure to take small bites and to chew this mochi thoroughly — if you do so, you should be fine! I've never had a problem chewing pounded mochi, but it is always wise to be careful.

Q: Do I need special tools to make or eat pounded mochi?

A: You can prepare pounded mochi in the comfort of your own home using a wooden mallet and a strong wooden or metal bowl, or a stand mixer with a paddle attachment. Granted, the mochi may not be as smooth if it is not made in a mochi machine, but it will still be smooth enough to eat and enjoy.

Q: Can I buy pounded mochi to use in some of the recipes in this book?

A: If you don't have time to pound your own mochi, you can easily buy kiri mochi, which is a commercially made pounded mochi available online or at Japanese grocery stores. It comes in rectangular pieces. Use it to make Yaki Mochi with Sweet Soy Sauce (page 114) and Bacon-Wrapped Mochi (page 116).

MOCHITSUKI
A New Year Mochi-Making Tradition

Mochitsuki is the Japanese tradition of pounding rice into mochi. Mochi rice, or mochigome, is soaked overnight to soften it, steamed the next day, then pounded. A mochitsuki can take place in various ways — the mochi can be pounded ceremonially at a festival or family gathering, or it can be simply pounded in a mochi machine at home.

The most traditional method of mochitsuki involves pounding the steamed sweet rice in a very large bowl, called an *usu*, carved out of wood or granite. The day before a mochitsuki, the usu is typically filled with water. The following morning, the water is dumped out and replaced with hot water to warm the usu so the hot rice doesn't get cold while being pounded. Once the usu is adequately heated, the hot water is poured out and the steamed rice is put inside. Two people stand opposite each other and, using a sledgehammer-sized wooden mallet called a kine, begin to massage and smash the rice until it forms a large mass. At this point, the two people take turns pounding the mochi with their kine. A third person flips the mochi by hand after every few strokes, so that it is evenly pounded.

Eventually, the mochi becomes one big, sticky mound — you can no longer see individual grains of rice, and the mass is smooth and stretchy. This traditional style of mochitsuki can be done by families and relatives, who all gather together for a day of mochi making. Mochitsuki is also often performed at New Year's festivals, as it can be entertaining to watch the mochi being pounded.

POUNDED WHITE MOCHI

Hand-pounded mochi is the most traditional form of mochi; Japanese people have been preparing it this way for ages. For me, this form brings back memories of watching mochi being pounded during Japanese festivals in San Francisco, where I grew up. Every year, I watch my mother and her friend Emiko use the mochi machine to pound loads of mochi to distribute to family and friends as a New Year's gift. For this recipe, you'll need a large stainless steel or wooden bowl and a food-safe mallet, or a stand mixer with a paddle attachment. This recipe is easy to multiply for larger batches.

TIP: Soaking rice in water overnight before cooking will make it softer and easier to smooth and pound.

INGREDIENTS

2 cups Japanese sweet rice (see tip)

2 cups cold water for the rice cooker or 2¼ cups cold water for the stovetop

Cornstarch or Japanese potato starch, for dusting

YIELD:
10
PIECES

COOKING THE RICE IN A RICE COOKER

1. Pour the rice into the rice cooker bowl, fill the bowl with enough cold water to submerge the rice, then rub the rice together with your hands and swirl it around the bowl. This helps remove starches that can hinder the stickiness of the rice. Rinse two more times, each time discarding as much cloudy water as possible. Drain in a colander.

2. Add 2 cups of fresh cold water and the drained rice to the rice cooker bowl and cook using the standard white rice settings. When the rice is done, immediately scoop the rice from the rice cooker into a large stainless steel or wooden bowl.

COOKING THE RICE ON THE STOVETOP

1. Pour the rice into a large bowl, then fill the bowl with enough cold water to submerge the rice. Rub the rice together with your hands and swirl it around the bowl. This helps remove starches that can hinder the stickiness of the rice. Rinse two more times, each time discarding

as much cloudy water as possible before refilling the bowl with fresh water. Drain in a colander.

2. Transfer the drained rice to a medium pot, add 2¼ cups water, and cover. Bring to a gentle boil over medium heat, then reduce the heat to low and continue to cook until there is no water left, about 25 minutes. Turn off the heat and let the rice rest, lid on, for 15 minutes.

3. Scoop the rice into a large stainless steel or wooden bowl.

POUNDING THE RICE

1. **If using a mallet:** Pound the mochi in the bowl in an up-and-down motion (1A, next page), stopping after every few pounds to dip the mallet in a small bowl of water to moisten it and prevent sticking. Pound for 3 minutes, then fold and mix the mochi rice with a spatula or rice paddle. Continue pounding and folding until all parts of the

Recipe continues on next page

mochi are evenly pounded, 10 to 15 minutes. You should have one large, sticky, soft, and stretchy mound of mochi dough, and you should no longer be able to see individual grains of rice (1B, previous page). The mixture may look a bit grainy, but that is okay. When you hand-pound the rice, it's hard to get the perfect texture.

If using a stand mixer and paddle attachment: Place the cooked rice in the mixer bowl and, using the paddle attachment, mix on speed level 2 until you have one large, sticky, soft, and stretchy mound of uniformly pounded mochi dough, 10 to 15 minutes. Dough made in a stand mixer may be smoother than dough that is hand-pounded.

2. Generously dust a cutting board with cornstarch and place dough on top of the starch (2A). Cover your hands in cornstarch and roll the entire mass of mochi dough in cornstarch to cover completely (2B). Pinch golf ball–sized pieces of mochi off the larger mound (2C), until all the mochi has been parceled into 10 pieces. Use as desired (see suggested uses below), or let cool on the cutting board (2D) before placing in a container and storing in the freezer for up to 2 months.

SUGGESTED USES

Cool until firm, then use in savory preparations, such as Ozoni Soup (page 119), Yaki Mochi with Sweet Soy Sauce (page 114), or Bacon-Wrapped Mochi (page 116), or toast and top with sweet soy sauce.

Turn it into a sweet dessert while still warm: Fill each mochi ball with sweet red bean paste (page 56) and your choice of sliced fruit.

2A

2B

2C

2D

YAKI MOCHI WITH SWEET SOY SAUCE

Yaki mochi reminds me not only of the New Year (thanks to all the fresh mochi my mother makes) but also of my mother-in-law. She likes to toast these crispy, melting morsels in winter, when it's cold outside. When you bite into the mochi, it is crunchy on the outside but gooey on the inside — a perfect combination of textures made even tastier with the savory accent of soy sauce. Truly, yaki mochi with soy sauce is a perfect match made!

INGREDIENTS

- 2 pieces plain, hand-pounded mochi (see note) or 2 pieces store-bought kiri mochi
- 1 tablespoon soy sauce
- 1 tablespoon sugar
- 1 piece nori, cut in half (optional)

DIRECTIONS

1. Set a piece of aluminum foil on a toaster oven rack or on a rack centered in your oven. Set the toaster oven, or preheat the oven, to 350°F/180°C. Place the mochi squares on the foil, spacing them at least 2 to 3 inches apart (they will expand quite a bit). Bake for 8 to 10 minutes, until light brown, puffy, and toasted on top. They may become lopsided, but that's okay.

2. While the mochi is toasting, combine the soy sauce and sugar in a small bowl and stir until the sugar has dissolved.

3. Remove the mochi from the oven. Enjoy hot, or when cool enough to handle, wrap each mochi in a half sheet of nori. Dip the mochi in the soy sauce mixture and enjoy immediately.

YIELD:
2
SERVINGS

NOTE: If you use hand-pounded mochi, make sure it has cooled and hardened before toasting. It can also be taken directly out of the freezer and toasted.

BACON-WRAPPED MOCHI

This creation is a loose interpretation of Spam *musubi*, a popular Hawaiian snack consisting of a slice of Spam canned meat on top of a block of rice and wrapped in a piece of nori. In my version, bacon takes the place of Spam, and a hunk of gooey, stretchy mochi replaces the rice. As with Spam musubi, this dish is finished off with a super-quick caramelized teriyaki sauce — really, the cherry on top! I have received rave reviews of this simple snack. You can use either homemade pounded mochi or kiri mochi (see page 108).

GLAZE

1 tablespoon mirin

1 tablespoon sake

1 tablespoon soy sauce

2 teaspoons sugar

BACON MOCHI

4 strips sliced bacon (do not use thick-cut)

4 rectangles kiri mochi

⅓ cup water

DIRECTIONS

1. **For the glaze:** Whisk together the mirin, sake, soy sauce, and sugar in a small bowl until fully dissolved. Set aside.

2. **For the bacon mochi:** Wrap 1 strip of the bacon around the center of the mochi, trying not to overlap the ends of the strip too much. Repeat with the remaining 3 pieces bacon and kiri mochi or homemade mochi.

3. Place the wrapped mochi, bacon edges seam down, in a medium skillet with a lid. Space the pieces at least 1½ inches apart. Add the water to the skillet. Cover and cook over medium-high heat until all the water in the pan evaporates, about 3 minutes. Continue to cook the mochi until the bacon looks seared and golden brown on the bottom. Flip the mochi over and cook for another minute, or until the mochi is soft and the bacon is golden brown on the other side. At this point, the mochi should be soft enough that you can pierce it all the way through the middle with a chopstick or fork. If it is not, add 1 tablespoon of water to the pan and continue to cook until the pan is sizzling and the mochi can be poked all the way through.

YIELD:
4
PIECES

4. Add the prepared glaze to the pan, coating the mochi. Cook for about 10 seconds, then flip the mochi and let the glaze caramelize on the other side, about 10 seconds longer. Do not allow the mochi to stay in the pan for more than 1 minute or the glaze will start to burn. Transfer to a plate, let cool for a minute, and enjoy warm.

OZONI SOUP
(SAVORY NEW YEAR'S MOCHI SOUP)

A light, clear soup with notes of dashi (a savory broth) and soy sauce, ozoni is a dish I most associate with the coming of each new year. My mother makes it every year around January 1, and our family enjoys this mochi soup together, using our freshly made mochi. Because mochi is stretchable and can be pulled into long strands, much like melted mozzarella, it represents longevity. Local produce is added to the soup as a prayer for a bountiful harvest in the new year. Feel free to double the amount of mochi pieces to serve very hungry guests.

NOTE: For a vegan-friendly version, don't include the chicken, bonito flakes, soy sauce, mirin, sake, or sugar. Instead, stir and fully dissolve ½ cup of white miso paste into the stock and simmer for 5 minutes before serving.

DASHI STOCK

- 4 dried shiitake mushrooms
- 1 small sheet kombu
- ¼ cup bonito flakes
- 5 cups water

SOUP

- 5 cups water
- 2 pounds bone-in chicken thighs, skin-on or skinless
- 1 cup ½-inch peeled, sliced moons daikon radish
- 1 carrot, peeled and sliced into ½-inch half-moons
- 4 tablespoons soy sauce
- 2 tablespoons mirin
- 2 tablespoons sake
- 1½ tablespoons sugar
- 2 teaspoons salt, plus more to taste
- 10 pieces pounded mochi

TOPPINGS (OPTIONAL)

Thinly sliced scallions

Cooked mature spinach, cooled, squeezed, and sliced into 2-inch-long bunches

Sliced carrots and daikon radishes

YIELD:
8–10
SERVINGS

Recipe continues on next page

OZONI SOUP

DIRECTIONS

1. **For the dashi stock:** Add the mushrooms, kombu, bonito flakes, and water to a large pot. Place over medium-low heat and simmer for 20 minutes. Strain the mushrooms, kombu, and bonito from the stock. The dashi stock is now done. Reserve the mushrooms, removing the stems, and slice the caps into thin strips to use as garnish later. To make more dashi for another recipe, reserve the remaining dashi ingredients in a container and cover with water, saving it in the refrigerator.

2. **For the soup:** Pour the dashi stock into a large pot. Add the water and bring to a boil over high heat. Add the chicken thighs and reduce the heat to medium-low. Simmer for 30 minutes, skimming off any foam from the surface of the soup while it cooks.

3. Add the daikon and carrot slices to the pot. Simmer for 30 minutes.

4. Remove the chicken thighs from the soup. Once cool enough to handle, pull the meat from the bones and roughly shred. Reserve the shredded chicken for topping.

5. Stir the soy sauce, mirin, sake, sugar, and salt into the soup, and simmer for 10 minutes.

6. If using freshly pounded mochi, place 1 or 2 pieces in each bowl and ladle the soup over them. If using frozen, refrigerated, or store-bought mochi, cook it in a separate pot of boiling water until soft, about 4 minutes, before placing pieces in the soup bowls and ladling soup over them.

7. Top each serving with some shredded chicken, mushrooms, scallions, cooked spinach, and sliced carrots and daikon radishes if using.

TIP: You can find cute flower- and star-shaped cookie cutters online.

ODANGO:
Balls of Fun

Odango are balls of mochi typically boiled for several minutes until fully cooked, then shocked in ice water to create a final, chewy bite. Odango go well in many desserts where you would like a quick bite of mochi texture. They can be served atop sundaes, eaten with ice cream and sweet red bean paste for a satisfying treat, put into hot soups like *zenzai* (page 135), skewered onto sticks and painted with a sweet soy glaze, or simply dipped in a sweet matcha or chocolate syrup. After you try some of these recipes, feel free to venture into your own odango experiments.

ODANGO Q & A

Q: Do you need skewers to serve odango?

A: Odango are often enjoyed skewered on 5- to 6-inch-long sticks, three balls per stick, but they can be enjoyed on their own, with sauce slathered on top of each ball, or served as hors d'oeuvres with a toothpick stuck into each ball of dango.

Q: What's the difference between odango and dango, and why are both terms used?

A: *Odango* is a feminine, more formal name, and *dango* is a masculine term. For example, in Japan a woman would call this dish "odango," while a man might call it the harsher-sounding "dango." Similarly, a woman would call mochi "omochi" while a man would simply call it "mochi." Also, if there is a descriptor in front of the word, it changes from *odango* to *dango* ("matcha dango," for instance). For this reason, the recipes in this section generally use the form *dango* instead of *odango*.

Q: Are there many ways to make odango?

A: In this chapter, I show two ways to make odango: one with mochiko and water and the other with silken tofu, water, and mochiko. However, there are other, more formal ways to make odango. Some recipes use an equal combination of regular Japanese rice flour (*joshinko*) and sticky Japanese rice flour (*shiratamako*). I simply use mochiko and water because that's the way my Japanese friends and family taught me to make odango, and I'm used to eating odango that are made this way.

PLAIN DANGO

This is a great, simple alternative to Tofu Dango (page 126). Note, however, that I recommend tofu dango for all the recipes in this book that require odango. Plain dango is a bit denser and chewier than tofu dango. Use these balls on top of sundaes and ice cream, or with mitarashi sauce (page 128), matcha sauce (page 133), or black sesame sauce (page 129). You'll need ten small (5- to 6-inch) wooden skewers.

INGREDIENTS

1½ cups mochiko, plus more as needed

4 tablespoons sugar, plus more as needed

⅛ teaspoon salt

¾ cup water

Ice cubes, for ice bath

Sauce of choice

DIRECTIONS

1. Whisk together the mochiko, sugar, and salt in a medium bowl until well blended.

2. Add the water and, using your hands, mash the ingredients together until completely blended and uniform in texture. The mixture should look and feel like a smooth playdough. If it is cracking a lot, it is too dry; add 1 teaspoon of water and mash together thoroughly. If it is too sticky, add more mochiko in 1- to 2-teaspoon increments until smooth.

3. Wet your hands. Pinch off small pieces of the dough and roll into 1½-inch balls. Form more balls until all of the dough is gone. Aim to make around 30 balls.

4. Fill a large bowl with ice water and set aside for an ice bath. Bring a large pot of water to a boil over high heat. When the water is boiling, add the odango. Cook until they rise to the surface, about 2 minutes, then cook for 2 minutes longer. Do not exceed 4 minutes total boiling time, even if they do not all rise.

5. Remove all the dango balls with a strainer or slotted spoon and transfer to the ice bath for 2 to 3 minutes. Drain the dango well. Skewer three balls on each stick and cover with your choice of sauce.

YIELD:
8-10
SKEWERS

TOFU DANGO

My mother shared this recipe, which was developed by one of her friends. I've tweaked it to create a flavorful dango that is soft but still provides a chewy bounce. These odango can be skewered onto sticks or simply slathered in a sauce and eaten with toothpicks, like an appetizer. If you cannot have soy, I recommend the Plain Dango recipe (page 125) instead. This simple recipe makes dango balls that can be used in mitarashi dango (page 128), with the matcha sauce (page 133), or with black sesame sauce (page 129). The tofu taste is very light, so it's not immediately obvious that tofu is an ingredient.

INGREDIENTS

- 1 cup mochiko, plus more as needed
- 4 ounces silken tofu, drained, such as House Foods premium soft
- 3 tablespoons water, plus more as needed
- 3 tablespoons sugar
- ⅛ teaspoon salt
- Ice cubes, to make an ice bath
- Sauce of choice

YIELD:
6–7
SKEWERS

DIRECTIONS

1. Combine the mochiko, tofu, water, sugar, and salt in a medium bowl. Using your hands, mash and mix the ingredients together until thoroughly blended. The mixture should look and feel like smooth playdough. Form a 1-inch ball with your hands; if the dough ball is cracking, mix in more water by the teaspoon until the dough has a smooth texture when rounded into a ball. The dough should be easy to roll into small balls. If it feels too wet, is not easy to roll, or sticks a lot to your hands, mix in additional mochiko by the teaspoon until it reaches the desired texture.

2. Pinch off small pieces of the dough and roll into 1-inch balls. Form more balls until all of the dough is gone.

3. Fill a large bowl with ice water and set aside for your ice bath. Bring a medium pot of water to a boil over high heat. When the water is boiling, add the odango. Cook until they rise to the surface, about 2 minutes, then cook for 2 minutes longer. Do not exceed 4 minutes total cooking time, even if they do not all rise.

ODANGO WITH
SWEET SOY SAUCE
(page 128)

4. Remove all the dango balls with a strainer or slotted spoon and transfer to the ice bath for 2 to 3 minutes. Drain the dango well. Skewer three or four balls on a small bamboo skewer. Continue until all the balls have been skewered. Cover with your sauce of choice.

SWEET SOY SAUCE (MITARASHI DANGO)

Mitarashi dango is the type of odango that you may be most familiar with because it is almost always present in Japanese convenience stores. Three white dango mochi balls are covered in a sauce that has the unctuous umami taste of soy sauce accented with sweetness from sugar. The satisfying chewiness of the mochi balls combined with the sweet and savory sauce makes for a perfect snack. Pair this sauce with Tofu Dango or Plain Dango. For best results, use a pastry brush to apply the sauce to the dango.

INGREDIENTS

- ½ cup water
- 3 tablespoons sugar
- 1 tablespoon soy sauce
- 1 tablespoon mirin
- 2 teaspoons cornstarch
- 1 batch Tofu Dango (page 126) or Plain Dango (page 125)

DIRECTIONS

1. Combine the water, sugar, soy sauce, mirin, and cornstarch in a medium saucepan. Whisk well, until all of the cornstarch is dissolved into the liquid.

2. Set the pan over medium heat. Simmer, whisking continually, until the sauce becomes thick and glossy.

3. Immediately remove the sauce from the heat.

4. Place the odango on skewers, then brush the sauce over the odango. Slide the skewers under your oven broiler for a minute, or use a culinary torch to lightly brûlée them. The odango will taste delicious grilled, with a caramelization from the sugar in the sauce.

YIELD:
8-10
SKEWERS

BLACK SESAME SAUCE

This black sesame sauce is nutty, complex, and super satisfying on top of chewy odango balls, accompanied by hot tea. The kinako is optional so don't worry if you can't find it, but it will improve the flavor. You'll need a clean spice grinder or mortar and pestle for this recipe. I would like to thank my friend Eri Combs from Eri's Bakery for helping to develop this recipe.

INGREDIENTS

- ½ **cup roasted black sesame seeds**
- 4 **tablespoons honey**
- 4 **tablespoons water**
- 1 **teaspoon sesame oil**
- 2 **tablespoons packed brown sugar**
- ⅛ **teaspoon salt**
- 2 **tablespoons kinako (optional)**
- 1 **batch Plain Dango (page 125) or Tofu Dango (page 126)**

DIRECTIONS

1. Grind the sesame seeds in a spice grinder or mortar and pestle until crumbled into a powder.

2. Combine the powdered seeds, honey, water, oil, brown sugar, salt, and kinako (if using) in a medium bowl. Whisk until completely smooth.

3. Place the odango on skewers, then generously brush or spoon the sauce over the odango.

YIELD:
4
SKEWERS

SANSHOKU DANGO

Sanshoku or "three-color" dango is usually served at teatime with a cup of hot Japanese green tea. I remember seeing these in stores while travelling in Japan and thinking how pretty the three colors — pink, white, and green — looked together. Sanshoku dango can also be called *hanami* dango when it is served during the spring cherry blossom season because pink, white, and green represent spring colors.

If you don't want to use food coloring, you can substitute ¼ teaspoon food-grade beet powder to make the pink dango. You'll need ten small wooden skewers. For extra flavor, brush on Sweet Soy Sauce (page 128) or Matcha Sauce (page 133).

INGREDIENTS

- 2 cups mochiko, plus more as needed
- 4 ounces silken tofu, drained, or ¼ cup water
- ¼ cup water, plus more as needed
- 3 tablespoons sugar
- ⅛ teaspoon salt
- 1 teaspoon matcha, sifted
- 1 drop liquid red food coloring
- Ice cubes, to make an ice bath

DIRECTIONS:

1. Combine the mochiko, tofu, water, sugar, and salt in a medium bowl. Using your hands, mash and mix the ingredients together until thoroughly blended. The mixture should look and feel like smooth, soft playdough. If it is cracking, add 1 teaspoon of water and mix again. If it looks too wet, add 1 to 2 teaspoons or more of mochiko.

2. Divide the mixture equally into three different bowls. In one bowl, mix the matcha with the dough. In another bowl, mix the red food coloring with the dough. Leave the final dough uncolored. Mix each colored dough very thoroughly by mashing together with your hands until the color is consistent throughout each dough.

3. Working with one dough at a time, pinch off small pieces of dough and roll into 1-inch balls. Form more odango balls until all of the dough is gone.

4. Fill a large bowl with ice water and set aside for your ice bath. Bring a medium pot of water to a boil over high heat. When the water is boiling, add the odango. Cook

until they rise to the surface, about 2 minutes, stirring occasionally to prevent the balls from sticking to the bottom of the pot. Once they rise, cook for 2 minutes longer. Do not exceed 4 minutes total boiling time, even if they do not all rise.

5. Remove the dango balls with a strainer or slotted spoon and transfer to the ice bath for 2 to 3 minutes. Drain the dango well. Skewer three balls on each stick in the following order: green, white, then pink.

YIELD:
10
SKEWERS

MATCHA DANGO WITH MATCHA SAUCE

This recipe is a twist on the traditional mitarashi dango recipe (page 128), using a simple matcha sauce instead of the mitarashi sauce. This recipe was inspired by my friend Eri Combs, a Japanese baker at Eri's Bakery. You'll need eight to ten small wooden skewers.

MATCHA ODANGO

1½ cups mochiko, plus more as needed

4 tablespoons sugar

2 teaspoons matcha, sifted

⅛ teaspoon salt

¾ cup plus 1 tablespoon water, plus more as needed

MATCHA SAUCE

¼ cup sugar

2 teaspoons cornstarch

1 teaspoon matcha, sifted

½ cup water

DIRECTIONS

1. **For the odango:** Whisk together the mochiko, sugar, matcha, and salt in a medium bowl until well blended.

2. Add the water and, using your hands, mash the ingredients together until completely blended and uniform in texture and light green color. The mixture should look and feel like smooth, soft playdough. If it is cracking a lot, it is too dry; add 1 teaspoon of water and mash together thoroughly. If it is too sticky, add more mochiko in 1- to 2-teaspoon increments.

3. Wet your hands. Pinch off small pieces of the dough and roll into 1-inch balls. Form more balls until all of the dough is gone. Aim to make around 30 balls; if you have extra, that is fine.

4. Fill a large bowl with ice water and set aside for your ice bath. Bring a large pot of water to a boil over high heat. When the water is boiling, add the odango. Cook until they rise to the surface, about 2 minutes, then cook for 2 minutes longer. Do not exceed 4 minutes total boiling time, even if they do not all rise.

YIELD:
8-10
SKEWERS

Recipe continues on next page

5. Remove all the odango balls with a strainer or slotted spoon and transfer to the ice bath for 2 to 3 minutes. Drain the odango well. Skewer three balls on each stick.

6. **For the sauce:** Whisk together the sugar, cornstarch, and matcha in a small microwavable bowl. Add the water and whisk until there are no lumps. Microwave for 1 minute, then stir. Microwave for an additional 30 seconds and stir once more.

7. Arrange the skewered odango on a plate and, using a pastry brush, generously brush the sauce over all of the odango. If you don't have a pastry brush, simply spoon the sauce over the odango.

VARIATION: *Want to incorporate tofu? Replace the water with 6 ounces of drained silken tofu and mash together well.*

ZENZAI SOUP WITH ODANGO
(SWEET RED BEAN SOUP WITH MOCHI BALLS)

This dessert soup is simple yet satisfying. The addition of tofu imbues the odango with a unique flavor and softness, making it highly enjoyable. The flavor and texture of warm, earthy-sweet adzuki beans and soft, chewy mochi balls are incredibly pleasing and comforting when eaten together. Zenzai mochi soup is most commonly enjoyed during the colder months.

INGREDIENTS

- 1 (17.6-ounce/ 500 g) package red bean (anko) paste, or 2 cups homemade red bean paste (page 56)
- 2 cups water
- 1 batch uncooked Tofu Dango (page 126)

DIRECTIONS

1. Stir the bean paste and water together in a medium pot over medium heat. Bring the soup to a boil.

2. Stir in the uncooked dango balls and lower the heat to a simmer. Cook for 2 minutes, stirring occasionally. Once the odango float to the top, cook for 2 minutes longer. Do not exceed 4 minutes total cooking time, even if they do not all rise.

3. Ladle the soup into bowls, placing four or five odango in each bowl. Serve hot.

YIELD: 5-6 SERVINGS

MATCHA ANMITSU WITH MANGO DANGO

Anmitsu is the perfect summer dessert. The dish's varied components provide for a delicious textural experience: Mango mochi balls are topped with ice cream, sweet red bean paste, fresh fruit, and matcha cubes, then finished with a brown sugar syrup. These ingredients can be plated in a fancy way, or simply arranged in a bowl. This recipe was created by Mutsumi Niwa, a talented Japanese mochi and wagashi maker who posts her creations regularly to a blog called Sakura Junction. Mutsumi sells her wagashi and teaches classes at Havan, a boutique and matcha bar in London. You can use Plain Dango (page 125) instead of the mango dango.

MATCHA AGAR CUBES

- 3 teaspoons matcha, sifted
- 2 tablespoons water
- 1¼ cups boiling water
- ½ teaspoon agar powder
- 4 tablespoons granulated sugar

BROWN SUGAR SYRUP (OPTIONAL)

- 2 tablespoons packed dark brown sugar
- 1 tablespoon water

MANGO DANGO MOCHI BALLS

- ½ cup mochiko
- 2 teaspoons granulated sugar
- ¼ cup mango juice (fresh or store-bought)

ADDITIONAL TOPPINGS

- ½ cup coarse sweet red bean paste (page 56)
- 4 scoops vanilla or green tea ice cream

  Sliced mango cubes, sliced strawberries, or other seasonal fruits (optional)

YIELD:
4
SERVINGS

Recipe continues on next page

MATCHA ANMITSU

DIRECTIONS

1. **For the agar cubes:** Mix the matcha with 1 tablespoon of the water in a small bowl. Press out all the lumps with a spatula; when it becomes smooth, add another 1 tablespoon of water to make a thinner texture. Set aside.

2. Pour the boiling water into a medium microwavable bowl. Add the agar and mix well. Microwave on high until it starts boiling, about 1 minute, then stir well to dissolve the agar. If the agar is still visible, heat it again until agar is completely dissolved and the mixture becomes completely clear. You should not be able to see any grains of the powder.

3. Once the agar has dissolved completely, stir in the granulated sugar. Microwave until the sugar has dissolved completely, about 30 seconds. Add the reserved matcha paste to the agar syrup and whisk well.

4. Pour the mixture into a small rectangular container, such as a 4- by 8-inch rectangular glass container. The agar should go an inch up the side of the container. Let the mixture cool at room temperature until it solidifies, then refrigerate for at least 1 hour. Place 4 small serving bowls in the refrigerator as well.

5. **For the brown sugar syrup (optional):** Mix the brown sugar and water in a small microwavable bowl. Microwave on high for 1 minute, stir, then microwave for another 30 seconds and stir again. Use oven mitts or a kitchen towel when handling the bowl, as it will be very hot. The quantity should reduce slightly and become a thin, syrupy consistency. Be careful not to let the liquid bubble up over the container. Cool at room temperature. The syrup can be kept in the refrigerator for about a month.

6. **For the mochi balls:** Stir together the mochiko and granulated sugar in a small bowl. If using fresh mango, make juice by pushing the fruit through a sieve. Add the mango juice to the mochiko and knead well with a spatula to eliminate lumps. Mix until the dough is smooth and able to be rolled in your hands. Divide the dough into 20 equal pieces, and roll them into small balls of about 1 inch in diameter.

7. Fill a large bowl with ice water and set aside for your ice bath. Bring a medium pot of water to a boil over medium heat. When it starts to boil, reduce the heat to medium-low heat and maintain a simmer. Add all the odango to the pot. Cook until they rise to the surface, about 2 minutes, stirring once or twice to prevent the balls from sticking to the bottom of the pot. Once they rise, cook for 1 minute longer. It should take a total of 3 minutes cooking time. Do not overcook or the balls will get too soft. Cut one ball in half to ensure it is fully cooked, with a uniform consistency throughout.

8. Remove all the odango balls with a strainer or slotted spoon and transfer to the ice bath for 2 to 3 minutes. Stir to separate any balls that are stuck together. Drain the odango well. Odango balls may harden if kept in the fridge. It's best if they are made just before serving.

9. **For assembly:** Remove the agar gel from the fridge and cut into cubes. Remove the serving bowls from the refrigerator and spoon agar cubes into the bottom of each. Add 1 tablespoon of the coarse sweet red bean paste on top of the gelatin. Place 1 scoop of ice cream next to the ball of bean paste, then top with 4 or 5 mango mochi balls. If desired, arrange slices of fresh strawberry and chopped mango next to the sweet red bean paste. Finally, drizzle some brown sugar syrup on top and serve.

7

BAKED MOCHI

I use my days off from teaching mochi classes to research and discover mochi dishes that go beyond traditional mochi and sweet daifuku mochi. I've particularly enjoyed doing research in the Bay Area, a hot spot for new food ideas, as well as in Hawaii, where mochi has been popular for quite some time. As it turns out, delicious baked goods can be made from mochi flour, eggs, sugar, and milk! They are gluten-free and have a somewhat mochi-like texture, yet they still have the familiar taste of baked goods. My hope is that this chapter provides you with lots of delicious baked mochi dishes and also inspires unique creations of your own.

BAKED MOCHI Q & A

Q: **Where did baked mochi originate?**

A: Baked mochi cupcakes and pancakes are more recent trends, due to the rising popularity of gluten-free diets and mochi products in general. However, one baked mochi dish called *chi chi dango* is believed to have initially made its appearance in Hawaii.

Q: **Does baked mochi keep for longer than steamed mochi?**

A: Yes. Since this mochi has stabilizers such as eggs and milk and isn't often filled, it is more shelf stable than steamed mochi. Note, however, that the baked mochi recipes in this chapter are best eaten fresh — on the same day they are baked. They will be fine the next day, but mochi in general tends to harden when exposed to the cold. I have found that recipes without custard or pudding, such as the Coconut Chi Chi Dango (page 166) and the Matcha–White Chocolate Mochi Brownies (page 174), can be stored in an airtight container at room temperature for up to 2 days and still taste good. Of course, on a hot day, it is better to place mochi in a cooler spot so it doesn't spoil.

KURI MANJU
(BAKED BUNS WITH SWEET BEAN FILLING)

INGREDIENTS

2½ cups sweet red or white bean paste (pages 56 and 58)

4¼ cups all-purpose flour, plus more as needed and for dusting

2 teaspoons baking powder

1 teaspoon baking soda

1 cup sugar

½ cup (1 stick) unsalted butter

2 large whole eggs

2 tablespoons egg whites (from 1 egg)

2 tablespoons light corn syrup, such as Karo

½ cup evaporated milk

EGG WASH

2 large egg yolks

1 teaspoon soy sauce

1 teaspoon mirin

YIELD:
50
PIECES

Manju is a type of sweet bean-filled pastry, and this one features sweet red or white bean paste. These manju are soft and delicious, with a beautiful color. Creating them can be a bit time consuming, so get some helping hands! The recipe comes from Mrs. Yukiko Otake, a lovely Japanese lady who has been perfecting this recipe for 10 years. I feel so blessed to be given this wisdom from Yuki-san, and to have her permission to share this recipe with you. You'll need a stand mixer fitted with a paddle attachment or a hand mixer and a large bowl, as well as a fine-mesh sieve.

DIRECTIONS

1. Roll the bean paste into 50 balls of about 1 tablespoon each. Refrigerate or freeze the balls in an airtight container until ready to use.

2. With a rack in the middle of the oven, preheat the oven to 350°F/180°C.

3. Whisk together the flour, baking powder, and baking soda in a medium bowl. Set aside.

4. In the bowl of a stand mixer (or a large bowl if using a hand mixer), cream the sugar and butter on medium-high speed until fluffy and lighter in color, 3 to 4 minutes.

5. Reduce the mixer speed to medium. Add the whole eggs one at a time, mixing to incorporate well after each addition. With the mixer running, gradually add the egg whites and mix for 1 minute. Add the corn syrup and mix for 1 minute longer.

6. Reduce the mixer speed to low. Alternate adding the flour mixture in four parts and evaporated milk in three

Recipe continues on next page

KURI MANJU

parts, starting and ending with the flour (it turns out better to end with flour). Mix on low until just incorporated — do not overmix. If the dough sticks to your hands, mix just enough flour to handle the dough without it being too sticky, up to 2 tablespoons (too much flour will make the manju tough).

7. To form the manju, pinch off a tablespoon-sized piece from the dough. Roll into a ball (7A), then use the palm of your hand to flatten it between two pieces of parchment paper until you have a ¼-inch-thick circle (7B). Place a ball of

bean paste in the center (7C). It's better to avoid using any additional flour during this process, but if the dough is too sticky, dust your hands very lightly with flour to help mold the dough.

8. Gently close the flat dough circle around the bean paste ball (8A), making sure there are no air pockets, and apply gentle pressure to seal the outer layer around the filling (8B). Shape the manju into an oval shape and pinch the sides slightly to form a base (8C), allowing the manju to stand on its own; this is important for the baking process.

Recipe continues on next page

9. Space the manju 2 inches apart on baking sheets lined with parchment paper, about 10 pieces per sheet. Continue until all the dough and filling have been used.

10. Create an egg wash by beating together the 2 egg yolks, soy sauce, and mirin with a fork. Strain this through a fine-mesh sieve (optional), using a spoon to push it through (this removes any lumps, making the wash easier to apply). Using a pastry brush, brush the egg wash onto the top of each manju, brushing each one twice.

11. Bake for 15 to 20 minutes, rotating the baking sheets halfway through the baking time, until the manju are light golden brown. Let cool on the baking sheets on wire racks. Store the completely cooled manju in an airtight container at room temperature for the day, in the refrigerator for up to 5 days, or in the freezer for up to 2 weeks.

MOCHI CUPCAKES

Chewy, satisfying, and with a wholesomely sweet bite, these cupcakes will be the highlight of any potluck event you attend! This amazing recipe, developed by Eri Combs of Eri's Bakery, is delicious, and it tastes even more sensational with chocolate chips or other add-ins thrown in.

INGREDIENTS

- **1 cup mochiko**
- **1 teaspoon baking powder**
- **⅛ teaspoon salt**
- **3 tablespoons unsalted butter, softened**
- **3 tablespoons sugar**
- **2 tablespoons honey**
- **2 large eggs**
- **2 tablespoons whole-milk plain yogurt**
- **1 teaspoon pure vanilla extract**
- **⅓ cup whole milk**
- **½ cup sweet red bean paste (page 56) or Nutella (optional)**

DIRECTIONS

1. Preheat the oven to 325°F/170°C. Coat six cups of a muffin pan with cooking spray.

2. Sift together the mochiko, baking powder, and salt in a small bowl. Set aside.

3. Whisk the butter in a large bowl until fluffy. Add the sugar and honey, and whisk well until the mixture takes on a lighter color, about 2 minutes.

4. Beat in the eggs one at a time, whisking well after each addition, until the batter becomes smooth. Add the yogurt and vanilla, and whisk again. Stir in the reserved mochiko mixture and combine until smooth. Pour in the milk and whisk thoroughly one more time.

5. Pour the batter halfway up each muffin cup. Add a rounded 2-teaspoon ball of sweet red bean paste or 1 teaspoon of spread to each cup, if using, then cover with 2 tablespoons of batter, making sure you can't see any of the filling.

6. Bake for 25 minutes, or until golden brown.

VARIATIONS: *For* **Matcha Mochi Cupcakes**, *replace the vanilla extract with 1½ teaspoons of matcha.*

Before baking, sprinkle the cupcakes with white and black sesame seeds for a beautiful look.

YIELD:

6

MUFFINS

JAPANESE-STYLE MOCHI CUPCAKES WITH SWEET RED BEAN FILLING

The recipe for these lighter-style mochi cupcakes comes from my mother's Japanese friend Keiko-san. Japanese baked goods are often less sweet and fluffier than typical American baked goods. These cupcakes are exactly that — pillowy, light, chewy, and slightly sweet. They are simply delicious! I remember eating these as a child whenever Keiko-san would bring them to community events. The sweet red bean paste on the inside is a fun surprise that pairs well with the soft cupcake.

INGREDIENTS

1½ **cups mochiko**

⅓ **cup sugar**

2 **teaspoons baking powder**

1 **cup whole milk**

⅓ **cup vegetable oil**

2 **large eggs**

½ **cup sweet red bean paste (page 56)**

YIELD:
12
STANDARD
OR
24
MINI
MUFFINS

DIRECTIONS

1. Preheat the oven to 350°F/180°C. Line one or two muffin pans with cupcake liners.

2. Whisk together the mochiko, sugar, and baking powder in a large bowl. Add the milk, oil, and eggs, and mix well until the batter is no longer clumpy.

Recipe continues on next page

2. Pour in the batter so each muffin cup is one-third full. Make 1-teaspoon-size balls of sweet red bean paste and drop one in the middle of each muffin cup.

3. Pour in additional batter, stopping ½ inch before the top of the cupcake liners.

4. Bake for 25 minutes for standard cupcakes or 15 minutes for mini cupcakes, or until light brown and the cupcake bounces back when pressed lightly with a finger. Enjoy immediately or store in an airtight container at room temperature for up to 1 day.

VARIATIONS: *Add 2 teaspoons of sifted matcha to the dry ingredients to make matcha-flavored cupcakes.*

Add 1½ teaspoons rose water to the wet ingredients to make rosewater-flavored cupcakes.

MOCHI PANCAKES

Satisfy the urge for pancakes with mochi pancakes! Lightly sweet and chewy, these tasty treats will not disappoint. Top the pancakes with fresh fruit, maple syrup or Matcha Syrup (page 171), and homemade whipped cream or yogurt for a beautiful breakfast.

INGREDIENTS

- 2 **large eggs**
- 3 **tablespoons sugar**
- 2 **tablespoons honey**
- ⅓ **cup whole milk**
- 2 **tablespoons whole-milk plain yogurt**
- 1 **teaspoon pure vanilla extract**
- 1 **cup mochiko**
- 1 **teaspoon baking powder**
- 3 **tablespoons unsalted butter, melted**
- 1 **tablespoon vegetable oil or butter, for the pan**

DIRECTIONS

1. Whisk together the eggs, sugar, and honey in a large bowl. Add the milk, yogurt, and vanilla, and mix well.

2. Using a fine-mesh strainer, sift the mochiko and baking powder into the bowl. Mix again. Pour in the melted butter and mix until everything is well incorporated, with no lumps.

3. Warm the oil in a nonstick skillet over medium-low heat. When the oil starts shimmering, pour ¼ cup batter for each pancake. If the batter doesn't immediately spread into a circle, form it into a circle with a spoon.

4. Cook until some bubbles are rising and popping at the surface, 1 or 2 minutes. Flip the pancakes and cook the other side for another minute.

5. Serve with your favorite pancake toppings.

VARIATION: *Replace the vanilla extract with 1½ teaspoons sifted matcha to make matcha mochi pancakes.*

YIELD:
7-8
SMALL PANCAKES

PLAIN MOCHI DONUTS

I love the satisfying chew of this donut. It is moist with a cakelike texture but also chewy like mochi. Delicious on its own, this donut can be paired with the glazes in this chapter to highlight classic Japanese flavors. You will fall in love with these baked mochi donuts, a healthier alternative to fried mochi donuts. My friend Eri Combs helped develop this recipe, which was inspired by the delicious mochi-themed pastries made by Third Culture Bakery in Berkeley, California.

The recipe is easily doubled or tripled. You'll need a donut baking pan (I use a Wilton nonstick pan that yields four-inch-wide donuts) and a piping bag.

INGREDIENTS

- 1 tablespoon unsalted butter (or cooking spray), for greasing the pan
- 1 cup mochiko
- 1 teaspoon baking powder
- ⅛ teaspoon salt
- 2 large eggs
- 3 tablespoons granulated sugar (see note on page 153)
- 2 tablespoons honey
- ⅓ cup whole milk
- 2 tablespoons of whole-milk plain yogurt
- 1 teaspoon pure vanilla extract
- 3 tablespoons unsalted butter, melted

DIRECTIONS

1. Preheat the oven to 350°F/180°C. Grease six cavities in a donut pan.

2. Sift together the mochiko, baking powder, and salt in a small bowl.

3. In a large bowl, whisk together the eggs, sugar, and honey. Add the milk, yogurt, and vanilla, and whisk thoroughly. Stir in the mochiko mixture, then add the butter and mix until fully combined.

4. Fill a piping bag with the batter. Pipe the dough three-quarters of the way up each cavity in the prepared baking pan.

5. Bake for 20 minutes, rotating the pan halfway through the cooking time to ensure even browning. Cool for 10 to 15 minutes, or until lukewarm in temperature, before glazing. Store at room temperature. Donuts are best eaten the same day or the day after they are baked. They can also be frozen and defrosted for 2 hours before eating.

YIELD:
6
DONUTS

NOTE: If you plan to glaze the donuts, omit the sugar in step 3 (but keep the honey!), as it will make the end result too sweet.

CHOCOLATE MOCHI DONUTS

This unctuous chewy chocolate mochi donut goes well with the light yet tasty Chocolate Donut Glaze (page 155). I definitely ate more than one! You'll need a donut baking pan (I use a Wilton nonstick donut pan that yields four-inch-wide donuts) and a piping bag. The recipe easily doubles.

INGREDIENTS

- 3 tablespoons unsalted butter, melted, plus more for the pan
- 1¼ cups mochiko
- ¼ cup unsweetened cocoa powder
- 1 teaspoon baking powder
- ⅛ teaspoon salt
- 2 large eggs
- 2 tablespoons sugar
- 2 tablespoons honey
- ½ cup whole milk
- 2 tablespoons of whole-milk plain yogurt
- 1 teaspoon pure vanilla extract

DIRECTIONS

1. Preheat the oven to 350°F/180°C. Generously grease six cavities in a donut pan.

2. Sift together the mochiko, cocoa, baking powder, and salt in a small bowl.

3. In a large bowl, whisk together the eggs, sugar, and honey. Add the milk, yogurt, and vanilla, and whisk again. Stir in the mochiko mixture, then add the butter and mix until fully combined. The batter will be thick and flow slowly.

4. Fill a piping bag with the batter. Pipe the dough three-quarters of the way up each cavity into the prepared baking pan.

5. Bake for 20 minutes, rotating the pan halfway through the cooking time to ensure even browning. Cool until lukewarm, 10 to 15 minutes, before glazing. Store at room temperature. Donuts are best eaten the same day or the day after they are baked. They can also be frozen and defrosted for 2 hours before eating.

YIELD:
6
DONUTS

TIP: If you are not going to glaze your chocolate donuts, I recommend piping half your batter into the donut molds, sprinkling ½ cup chocolate chips on top, and then piping the other half of the batter on top of the chocolate chips for added chocolate flavor.

MATCHA DONUT GLAZE

I discovered this recipe while developing a matcha glaze for the mochi donuts in my five-course mochi class. While testing recipes, I realized the combination of melted white chocolate truly elevates the flavor of matcha, making it taste lighter and brighter, yet retaining its characteristic earthy flavor. After glazing, you might sprinkle the donuts with black sesame seeds or colorful sprinkles for extra flair!

INGREDIENTS

- 1½ cups confectioners' sugar
- 1 teaspoon high-quality matcha, sifted
- 2 tablespoons unsalted butter
- ¼ cup (43 g) good-quality white chocolate chips, such as Ghirardelli
- 3 tablespoons half-and-half

YIELD:
GLAZE FOR
6
DONUTS

DIRECTIONS

1. Sift together the powdered sugar and matcha in a small bowl until even in consistency.

2. Place the butter in a medium microwavable bowl. Microwave on high until the butter is fully liquefied, about 15 seconds. Add the chocolate chips and microwave for another 20 seconds. Stir the mixture thoroughly until fully blended. If the chocolate is not fully melted, microwave for another 15 seconds, and mix until smooth. It is okay if the mixture looks grainy; this will resolve in the next step.

3. Thoroughly stir the powdered sugar mixture and the half-and-half into the chocolate mixture. Microwave for another 30 seconds, and mix until smooth. The glaze should be fairly thick but still loose enough to drizzle from a spoon. If it is too thick, add 1 extra teaspoon of half-and-half. If it is too thin, add 2 table-spoons of powdered sugar. If you are saving it for later, heat the glaze for 30 seconds and give it a stir before you start dipping the doughnuts. The glaze must be warm and the doughnuts at room temperature for the glazing process to work. (See the glazing instructions on page 156.)

4. Refrigerate extra glaze for 5 days or freeze for up to 3 weeks.

VARIATIONS: *For a* **Chocolate Donut Glaze***, substitute 1 tablespoon of unsweetened cocoa powder for the matcha, substitute semisweet chocolate chips for the white chocolate chips, and add ⅛ teaspoon salt when you combine the sugar and cocoa. You could also add 1 teaspoon peppermint extract for a minty chocolate glaze, 1 teaspoon orange extract for an orange-chocolate glaze, or 1 teaspoon cinnamon for a Mexican hot chocolate flavor.*

HOW TO GLAZE DONUTS

1. Remove the donuts from the baking mold and let cool to room temperature. If a donut is too warm (i.e., fresh out of the oven), the glaze will melt off of the donut, resulting in a lot of glaze on your plate and not much on the donut.

2. Make sure the glaze is warm and liquidy. If it has become too thick, warm it for 15 seconds in the microwave, then whisk. If the glaze appears dry after heating and doesn't flow when you move the bowl around, add up to 1 teaspoon of half-and-half or milk and whisk. Do not add too much milk or the glaze will not set properly. If the glaze gets too liquidy, simply add ½ cup powdered sugar to thicken it.

3. To glaze, pick up the donut with the lighter side facing up and the darker side facing down.

4. Dip the dark side into the warm glaze until the glaze reaches two-thirds of the way up the donut. Lift, then let the glaze drip for several seconds. Place the donut glaze side up on a wire rick or parchment paper until cool and the glaze is set.

TIP: To make your donut prettier, garnish with colorful sprinkles or melted high-quality white chocolate. To melt the white chocolate, combine it with a splash of neutral oil in a small bowl, then warm in the microwave for 30 seconds or more until melted. Use a fork to drizzle the chocolate on top of your finished glazed donut.

EARL GREY DONUT GLAZE

This recipe goes well on Plain Mochi Donuts (page 152) or Chocolate Mochi Donuts (page 154). I use Trader Joe's organic Earl Grey tea. You can really taste it in this glaze.

INGREDIENTS

- **4 tablespoons half-and-half**
- **2 Earl Grey tea bags, tags and staples removed**
- **¼ cup (43 g) good-quality white chocolate chips, such as Ghirardelli**
- **2 tablespoons unsalted butter, chopped**
- **⅛ teaspoon salt**
- **1½ cups confectioners' sugar**

DIRECTIONS

1. Measure 4 tablespoons of the half-and-half into a medium microwavable bowl. Add the tea bags, making sure to submerge the bags in the liquid. Microwave on high for 30 seconds. Stir the mixture a few times to help the tea steep into the half-and-half, being careful not to tear the tea bags while doing this. (It is preferable that no tea leaves get into the mixture.) Squeeze the tea bags to release their liquid into the bowl, and dispose of the bags. The half-and-half should turn a medium-dark brown color.

2. Add the white chocolate chips, butter, and salt to the infused half-and-half. Microwave until the chocolate and butter are melted, about 30 seconds, and whisk to dissolve any lumps. Stir in the sugar and mix thoroughly. Microwave for 30 seconds, and stir until no lumps are present. The glaze should be fairly thick but still loose enough to drizzle from a spoon. If it is too thick, add 1 extra teaspoon of half-and-half. If it is too thin, add ½ cup or more of powdered sugar.

YIELD:
GLAZE FOR
6
DONUTS

STRAWBERRY-ROSEWATER DONUT GLAZE

One of our popular dishes is the Rosewater Mochi (page 46). While making this mochi for a class one day, I filled it with strawberries and white chocolate. I found that rose water amplified the flavor of the strawberry, and the two paired perfectly together. This glaze tastes very much like strawberries yet has a delicate overtone of rose flavor. You'll need a clean spice grinder or mortar and pestle for this recipe.

INGREDIENTS

- ¼ **cup freeze-dried strawberries**
- 1½ **cups confectioners' sugar, sifted**
- 2 **tablespoons unsalted butter, chopped**
- ¼ **cup (43 g) good-quality white chocolate chips, such as Ghirardelli**
- 3 **tablespoons half-and-half**
- ½ **teaspoon rose water, such as Cortas brand**

DIRECTIONS

1. Spoon the strawberries into a spice grinder and grind into a fine powder. Measure 3 teaspoons of the powder into a small bowl and whisk in the powdered sugar until even in consistency. (Save any additional powder for another use.)

2. Place the butter in a medium microwavable bowl. Microwave on high until fully liquefied, about 15 seconds. Add the white chocolate chips and microwave for another 20 seconds. Stir the mixture thoroughly until fully blended. If the chocolate is not fully melted, microwave for another 15 seconds and mix until smooth. It is okay if the mixture looks grainy; this will resolve in the next step.

3. Thoroughly stir the powdered sugar mixture and the half-and-half into the chocolate mixture. Microwave for another 30 seconds, and mix until smooth. Add the rose water, and stir again until smooth. The glaze should be fairly thick but still loose enough to drizzle from a spoon. If it is too thick, add 1 extra teaspoon of half-and-half. If it is too thin, add ½ cup of powdered sugar. If you are saving it for later, be sure to heat the glaze for 30 seconds and give it a stir before you start dipping the donuts. The glaze must be warm and the donuts at room temperature for the glazing process to work. (See the glazing instructions on page 156.)

YIELD:
GLAZE FOR
6
DONUTS

KINAKO-CINNAMON DONUT GLAZE

This glaze screams "Fall is here!" The combination of kinako (earthy roasted ground soybeans) and cinnamon make it the perfect spice-flavored dessert to accompany hot cocoa or a fresh cup of pumpkin-spice coffee. The recipe is easily doubled or tripled.

INGREDIENTS

- 1½ cups confectioners' sugar
- 2 tablespoons kinako
- 1 teaspoon ground cinnamon
- 2 tablespoons unsalted butter, chopped
- ¼ cup (43 g) good-quality white chocolate chips, such as Ghirardelli
- 3 tablespoons half-and-half

DIRECTIONS

1. Sift together the powdered sugar, kinako, and cinnamon in a small bowl until evenly distributed.

2. Place the butter in a medium microwavable bowl. Microwave on high until the butter is fully liquefied, about 15 seconds. Add the chocolate chips and microwave for another 20 seconds. Stir the mixture thoroughly until fully blended. If the chocolate is not fully melted, microwave for another 15 seconds and mix until smooth. It is okay if the mixture looks grainy; this will resolve in the next step.

3. Thoroughly stir the powdered sugar mixture and the half-and-half into the chocolate mixture. Microwave for another 30 seconds, and mix until smooth. The glaze should be fairly thick but still loose enough to drizzle from a spoon. If it is too thick, add 1 extra teaspoon of half-and-half. If it is too thin, add 2 tablespoons of powdered sugar. If you are saving it for later, be sure to heat the glaze for 30 seconds and give it a stir before you start dipping the donuts. The glaze must be warm and the donuts at room temperature for the glazing process to work. (See the glazing instructions on page 156.)

YIELD:
GLAZE FOR
6
DONUTS

BLACK SESAME MOCHI DONUTS

Black sesame is a classic Japanese flavor. Nutty and with a slight savory twist, the flavor marries well with white chocolate, butter, and sugar, and makes an amazing treat paired with a chewy mochi donut. You'll need a donut baking pan (I use a Wilton nonstick pan that yields 4-inch-wide donuts), a clean spice grinder or mortar and pestle, and a piping bag. The recipe easily doubles or triples.

DONUTS

- 1 tablespoon unsalted butter (or cooking spray), for greasing the pan
- 4 tablespoons roasted black sesame seeds
- 1 cup mochiko
- 1 teaspoon baking powder
- ⅛ teaspoon salt
- 2 large eggs
- 2 tablespoons honey
- ⅓ cup whole milk
- 2 tablespoons whole-milk plain yogurt
- 1 teaspoon pure vanilla extract
- 3 tablespoons unsalted butter, melted

GLAZE

- 3 tablespoons roasted black sesame seeds
- 1½ cups confectioners' sugar
- 2 tablespoons unsalted butter, melted
- ¼ cup (43 g) good-quality white chocolate chips, such as Ghirardelli
- 3 tablespoons half-and-half
- Black sesame seeds, for decorating

YIELD:
6
DONUTS

Recipe continues on next page

BLACK SESAME DONUTS

1. **For the donuts:** Preheat the oven to 350°F/180°C. Generously grease six cavities in the donut pan.

2. Measure out 4 tablespoons of roasted black sesame seeds (see note on page 70) and grind in a spice grinder or mortar and pestle until fine. It may clump together towards the end; stop grinding when the clumping starts to occur.

3. Sift together the mochiko, sesame seeds, baking powder, and salt in a large bowl.

4. In a medium bowl, whisk together the eggs and honey. Stir in the milk, yogurt, and vanilla, and whisk thoroughly.

5. Add the egg mixture to the mochiko mixture, and whisk until fully incorporated and smooth. Pour in the melted butter, and mix until fully combined.

6. Fill a piping bag with the batter. Pipe the dough three-quarters of the way up each cavity into the prepared baking pan.

7. Bake for 20 minutes, rotating the pan halfway through the cooking time to ensure even browning. Cool for 10 to 15 minutes, or until lukewarm, before glazing.

8. **For the glaze:** While donuts are cooling, grind the sesame seeds, then combine with the sugar in a small bowl.

9. Place the butter in a medium microwavable bowl. Microwave on high until the butter is fully liquefied, about 15 seconds. Add the white chocolate chips and microwave for another 20 seconds. Stir the mixture thoroughly until fully blended. If the chocolate is not fully melted, microwave for another 15 seconds and mix until smooth. It is okay if the mixture looks grainy; this will resolve in the next step.

10. Thoroughly stir the sugar mixture and the half-and-half into the chocolate mixture. Microwave for another 30 seconds, and mix until smooth. The glaze should be fairly thick but still loose enough to drizzle from a spoon. If it is too thick, add 1 extra teaspoon of half-and-half. If it is too thin, add ½ cup of powdered sugar. If you are saving it for later, be sure to heat the glaze for 30 seconds and give it a stir before you start dipping the donuts. The glaze must be warm and the donuts at room temperature for the glazing process to work. (See the glazing instructions on page 156.)

11. After glazing each donut, lightly sprinkle on some black sesame seeds for a beautiful final look. Refrigerate extra glaze for 5 days or freeze for up to 3 weeks.

APPLE CIDER MOCHI DONUTS

DONUTS

- 1 tablespoon unsalted butter (or cooking spray), for greasing the pan
- 1 cup mochiko
- 1¼ teaspoons baking powder
- 1 teaspoon ground cinnamon
- 1 teaspoon apple pie spice
- ⅛ teaspoon salt
- 2 large eggs
- ¼ cup packed dark brown sugar
- ⅓ cup apple cider
- 2 tablespoons whole-milk plain yogurt
- 1 teaspoon pure vanilla extract
- 3 tablespoons unsalted butter, melted

Ingredients continued on next page

In fall I like to visit Lynd Fruit Farm near Columbus, Ohio, to go apple picking and purchase their delicious apple cider donuts. I decided to replicate the same apple cider taste, but in a mochi donut. The result is mouthwatering, addictive, and perfect with a hot beverage when the weather starts to cool in autumn. Note: These donuts must be eaten with the sugar-spice coating in order to taste great! You'll need a donut baking pan (I use a Wilton nonstick pan that yields 4-inch-wide donuts) and a piping bag. The recipe can be easily doubled or tripled.

DIRECTIONS

1. **For the donuts:** Preheat the oven to 350°F/180°C. Generously grease six cavities in a donut pan.

2. Sift together the mochiko, baking powder, cinnamon, apple pie spice, and salt in a large bowl.

3. In another large bowl, whisk together the eggs and brown sugar. Add the cider, yogurt, and vanilla, and whisk thoroughly.

4. Stir the egg mixture into the mochiko mixture, then add the butter and mix until fully incorporated and smooth.

5. Fill a piping bag with the batter. Pipe the dough three-quarters of the way up each cavity into the prepared baking pan.

YIELD:
6-10
DONUTS

1 cup granulated
  sugar

1 teaspoon ground
  cinnamon

1 teaspoon apple
  pie spice

6 tablespoons
  unsalted butter,
  melted

6. Bake 20 minutes, rotating halfway through the cooking time to ensure even browning, until golden brown, with a thin, crispy crust. When done, turn the donut pan upside down and flip the donuts out of the pan onto a wire rack. Cool until lukewarm, 10 to 15 minutes, before glazing.

7. For the coating: While the donuts are cooling, combine the granulated sugar, cinnamon, and apple pie spice in a small bowl and mix well. Put the melted butter in a separate bowl.

8. Working with one donut at a time, dip the donuts into the butter until completely coated, and then transfer to the cinnamon-sugar bowl and coat until completely covered. Store at room temperature. Donuts are best eaten the day they are baked; they may harden the next day.

COCONUT CHI CHI DANGO

INGREDIENTS

Canola oil or cooking spray, to grease the baking dish

1½ cups mochiko

⅔ cup sugar

¾ teaspoon baking powder

1 (13.5-ounce) can coconut milk, such as Chaokoh brand

⅔ cup water

3 tablespoons condensed milk

1 teaspoon pure vanilla extract

1 cup cornstarch or Japanese potato starch, for dusting

I first enjoyed chi chi dango on a trip to Honolulu with my husband and daughter. Not being from Hawaii, I didn't grow up with this treat, so the concept was foreign to me: mochi pieces without a filling? I was soon won over. The coconut chi chi dango I enjoyed at Fujiya Hawaii was the softest piece of mochi I had ever eaten, and it had a slightly sweet, addictive flavor I continued to crave afterward. Not just for coconut lovers, this is the perfect mochi dish to bring as light dessert bites for any barbecue or get-together. You'll need an eight-inch square baking dish for this recipe.

DIRECTIONS

1. Preheat the oven to 350°F/180°C. Grease a square 8-inch square baking dish.

2. Sift together the mochiko, sugar, and baking powder in a large bowl. Add the coconut milk, water, condensed milk, and vanilla, and stir until completely mixed and uniform in consistency.

3. Spread the mixture into the baking dish. It should go 1 inch up the sides of the dish, but no higher than 2 inches, as chi chi dango is supposed to bake as a sheet of mochi.

4. Bake for 45 minutes, or until the mochi is bubbly and a uniform color. If the middle looks slightly uncooked, bake 5 minutes longer or until the mixture looks uniform in texture.

5. Let cool to room temperature. Cut the mochi into strips 1 inch wide and 8 inches long, and dust each liberally with cornstarch to prevent from sticking.

YIELD:
25
BITE-SIZE
SQUARES

Cut each strip into thirds, to yield small mochi rectangles about 2½ inches long. Coat each piece in cornstarch, then shake or brush off the excess. Store in an airtight container at room temperature for up to 2 days; in hot weather, refrigerate after 1 day.

CHEWY MOCHI WAFFLES

I love waffles! There's nothing more satisfying than getting together with friends to mix up waffle batter and cook it on the griddle. These waffles are perfectly crispy with a slight mochi chew. They are delicious with a simple Matcha Syrup (page 171). Or try a topping of fresh-cut strawberries, syrup, a scoop of sweet red bean paste, and whipped cream — or the classic maple syrup. This recipe can easily be doubled and tripled.

INGREDIENTS

Cooking spray or unsalted butter, for coating the waffle grates

2¼ cups mochiko

4 teaspoons baking powder

⅛ teaspoon salt

⅓ cup plus 1 table-spoon sugar

1 large egg

1 cup coconut milk

½ cup milk

¼ cup vegetable oil

1 tablespoon unsalted butter, melted

2 teaspoons pure vanilla extract

¼ cup water

YIELD:
2-3
WAFFLES

DIRECTIONS

1. Whisk together 2 cups of the mochiko, the baking powder, and salt in a large bowl.

2. In another large bowl, mix together ⅓ cup of the sugar and the egg until blended, then add the coconut milk, milk, and oil, and blend until incorporated. Add the butter and vanilla. Mix until smooth.

3. Add the mochiko mixture to the sugar and milk mixture. Whisk thoroughly until smooth, 1 to 2 minutes.

4. Make a "mochi starter" by mixing together the remaining ¼ cup mochiko, the remaining 1 tablespoon sugar, and the water. Microwave on high for 1 minute. Add the starter directly to the batter and whisk until incorporated, about 2 minutes. The batter will look lumpy — that is fine.

5. Preheat a waffle maker on medium heat. Grease the grates.

6. Pour about 1 cup batter onto the waffle grate. Cook until lightly brown, 4 to 5 minutes. Grease the grate again before making another waffle.

VARIATIONS: For **Matcha Mochi Waffles**, *omit the vanilla and add 1 tablespoon matcha to the dry ingredients.*

For **Black Sesame Mochi Waffles**, *add 1 tablespoon ground roasted black sesame seeds (see note on page 70) to the dry ingredients.*

MATCHA SYRUP
(page 171)

CRISPY TOFU MOCHI WAFFLES

These tofu waffles are crisp on the outside with a chewy gooeyness on the inside. Light and easy to eat, they are on the healthier side because their main ingredient is tofu — but you'd never know it from the taste! These waffles bring back memories of visiting my friend's house in middle school. Her mother would make us vegan tofu waffles just like these that were super crispy and delicious.

INGREDIENTS

Cooking spray or unsalted butter, for coating the waffle grates

1½ cups mochiko

2 tablespoons sugar

1 teaspoon baking powder

¼ teaspoon salt

1 (14-ounce) container soft/silken tofu (I prefer House Foods brand), drained

½ cup water

¼ cup grapeseed, canola, or other neutral oil

YIELD:
3
WAFFLES

DIRECTIONS

1. Whisk together the mochiko, sugar, baking powder, and salt in a large bowl until thoroughly combined. Set aside.

2. Place the tofu, water, and oil in a blender and process until completely smooth. Scrape the tofu mixture into the mochiko mixture and whisk thoroughly until smooth.

3. Preheat a waffle maker on medium heat. Grease the grates.

4. Pour about ¾ cup batter onto the waffle grate. Cook until golden brown, 5 to 7 minutes. Grease the grate again before making another waffle.

MATCHA SYRUP

If you want something extra special on your mochi waffle or pancake, this matcha syrup is the answer! It packs a matcha punch and is the perfect alternative to traditional maple or pancake syrup.

INGREDIENTS

- 3 tablespoons packed brown sugar

- 1 teaspoon cornstarch

- 1 teaspoon ceremonial-grade matcha, sifted (see note)

- 3 tablespoons water

- 1 tablespoon (11 g) good-quality white chocolate chips, such as Ghirardelli

DIRECTIONS

1. Mix together the brown sugar, cornstarch, and matcha in a small microwavable bowl. Add the water and stir thoroughly, until the matcha and cornstarch have dissolved.

2. Microwave on high for 1 to 1½ minutes until the mixture starts to bubble and thicken. Add the chocolate chips and whisk until everything is combined. If the chocolate has not completely melted, microwave for 10 seconds longer, and whisk to combine once more.

> **NOTE:** The higher the quality of your matcha, the better this syrup will taste. Culinary-grade matcha will not produce as nice a flavor as ceremonial grade, especially for this kind of recipe, where you can really taste the matcha quality.

YIELD:
3
WAFFLES

CHOCOLATE MOCHI BROWNIES

Crispy on the outside and ooey-gooey mochi-licious on the inside, these brownies come together quickly and pack a serious chocolate punch! They are a perfect dessert or snack for when you get the nighttime munchies. Special thanks to my friend Yuki Peterson and her mother for inspiring this treat. You'll need a 9- by 13-inch baking dish for this recipe.

INGREDIENTS

Butter or neutral cooking oil for greasing pan

3 cups mochiko

½ cup unsweetened cocoa powder

1 tablespoon baking powder

½ teaspoon salt

2 large eggs

2 cups packed light brown sugar

2½ cups whole milk

½ cup vegetable oil

½ cup melted butter

2 teaspoons pure vanilla extract

1 cup semisweet chocolate chips

DIRECTIONS

1. Preheat the oven to 350°F/180°C. Grease a 9- by 13-inch baking pan.

2. Sift together the mochiko, cocoa, baking powder, and salt in a large bowl.

3. Beat the eggs in another large bowl. Stir in the sugar, milk, oil, butter, and vanilla. Mix well. Scrape this mixture into the bowl with the mochiko mixture and whisk until uniform in texture (make sure there are no lumps). Stir in ½ cup of the chocolate chips.

4. Pour the batter into the prepared pan, then scatter the remaining ½ cup chocolate chips on top.

5. Bake for 50 to 60 minutes, until golden brown. Enjoy hot with vanilla ice cream, or let cool to room temperature. Cut into squares and store in an airtight container at room temperature for 2 days, or in the freezer for up to 1 month.

YIELD:
10
PIECES

VARIATIONS:

Make **Black Sesame Mochi Brownies** *by grinding ¼ cup roasted black sesame seeds (see note on page 70) in a spice grinder, and replace the cocoa with the ground seeds plus 1 tablespoon kinako (optional but tasty); use 2 cups granulated sugar instead of the brown sugar, and swap white chocolate chips for the semisweet.*

For a nondairy alternative, replace cow's milk with a different type of milk and replace the butter with oil.

MATCHA-WHITE CHOCOLATE MOCHI BROWNIES

INGREDIENTS

Butter or neutral cooking oil for greasing pan

3 cups mochiko

2½ tablespoons matcha, sifted

1 tablespoon baking powder

½ teaspoon salt

2 large eggs

2 cups sugar

2½ cups whole milk

½ cup vegetable oil

½ cup melted butter

2 teaspoons pure vanilla extract

1 cup (170 g) good-quality white chocolate chips (Ghirardelli is best)

"Mochi mochi" is a term used in the Japanese language to describe a food that has a chewy, mochilike consistency. This brownie is chewy and crusty on the outside but mochilike on the inside, with little pockets of white chocolate! It is super good. You'll need a 9- by 13-inch baking pan for this recipe.

DIRECTIONS

1. Preheat oven to 350°F/180°C. Grease a 9- by 13-inch baking pan.

2. Sift together the mochiko, matcha, and baking powder in a large bowl.

3. Beat the eggs in another large bowl. Stir in the sugar, milk, oil, butter, and vanilla. Mix well. Scrape this mixture into the bowl with the mochiko mixture and whisk until uniform in texture (make sure there are no lumps). Mix in ½ cup of the chocolate chips.

4. Pour the batter into the prepared pan, then scatter the remaining ½ cup chocolate chips on top.

5. Bake for 60 minutes, or until golden brown. Best eaten warm, but also great at room temperature. Cut into squares and store in an airtight container at room temperature for 2 days.

YIELD:
10
PIECES

Thank You, Thank You, Thank You!

Thank you to my agent, Leslie Jonath, for believing in my vision for this book, and for working with great care to make it a reality. You fought hard to find an amazing publisher for this book, Storey Publishing, and I will forever be grateful. Your cheery spirit always uplifted and encouraged me so much during the process of writing this book.

Thank you, reader, for picking up this book! Please keep in touch with me on Instagram (@kaoriskitchen) and through e-mail (info@ kaoriskitchen.com). I would love to see your mochi creations (tag #mochimagic).

Thank you to the staff at Storey Publishing — Liz, Carolyn, Sarah, Anastasia, and more — for developing this book with excitement and hard work! Thank you to the amazing food stylist Jeffrey Larsen, assistant food stylist Natalie, photographer Wendi Nordeck, assistant photographer Afra, and my talented friend Koka Yamamoto! My experience making this book with you all is one I will never forget.

Thank you to my husband, Alan, for always listening to me rant about all my mochi recipes and inspirations. Thank you for being a wonderful dad, spouse, son, and brother, and thank you for inspiring me to be an entrepreneur and author and pushing me to pursue my dreams no matter how risky they seem initially. I'm very lucky to have you by my side. Thank you to my beloved daughter and forever mochi baby, Emilie, for showering us with lots of smiles and joy.

Thank you to my Heavenly Parent, and to my parents, Richard and Yukiko, who have raised me so well and continue to support and love me and my family. Thanks to my mother, Yukiko, for supporting my dreams of teaching cooking classes and helping them come true through daily support, last-minute babysitting, cleaning, teaching classes, recipe testing . . . the list goes on. Thanks to my sister, Rebecca, for always being a source of encouragement for my many and seemingly crazy ideas. Thank

you to the super-talented Gracie for your amazing photography and your constant encouragement, inspiration, and support. Your photos of my mochi inspired the creation of this book! Thank you to Yoko, Robert, and Harmony for tasting all of my mochi creations and giving me valuable feedback, and for watching Emilie while I wrote this book.

Thank you to my friend Claire Hallinan, for keeping me accountable to my goals every week while writing this book. You are a big reason this book exists today. A big thank you to Eri Combs of Eri's Bakery (erisbakery.com) for helping to test and develop many of the recipes in this book and assisting with mochi classes. Thank you to Yuki Otake, Haruko Nagaishi, and Mutsumi Niwa for your help in developing recipes for this book. Thank you to my friend and first draft editor Jinae Higashino for your thorough editing and Nathalie C. for your amazing edits as well as Carolyn Bonini for helping with final edits for the first draft of the book.

A big thank-you to all of my recipe testers! Thank you Junghwa Detlefsen, Janet Livingston, Carmen Shiu, Piper Murakami, Kathleen and Augustus Martin, Beverly Wong, Dan Oppenheimer, Tico Blumenthal, Marie Valmores, Mark Dessert, Diane Ruddle, Sora Stoll, Lara Voelker Shaw, Koreana Schmittat, Elizabeth Ramiro, Jill and Kim Nakamura and family, Haruko Nagaishi, Jean Bunac, Lance Akiyama, Marice Shiozaki, Lele Nguyen, Lorraine Chew, Madison Dickson, Audrey Martin, Tina Marie Lee, Yumiko Ishida, Michelle Ho, Jennifer Lee, Kimiko Marsi, Natascha Phillips, Emily Egusa, Karlin Bark, and many more tasters and testers (you know who you are!).

METRIC CONVERSION CHARTS

WEIGHT	TO CONVERT	TO	MULTIPLY
	ounces	grams	ounces by 28.35
	pounds	grams	pounds by 453.5
	pounds	kilograms	pounds by 0.45

LENGTH	TO CONVERT	TO	MULTIPLY
	inches	millimeters	inches by 25.4
	inches	centimeters	inches by 2.54
	inches	meters	inches by 0.0254
	feet	meters	feet by 0.3048
	feet	kilometers	feet by 0.0003048

VOLUME	TO CONVERT	TO	MULTIPLY
	teaspoons	milliliters	teaspoons by 4.93
	tablespoons	milliliters	tablespoons by 14.79
	fluid ounces	milliliters	fluid ounces by 29.57
	cups	milliliters	cups by 236.59
	cups	liters	cups by 0.24
	pints	milliliters	pints by 473.18
	pints	liters	pints by 0.473

INDEX

Page numbers in *italic* indicate photos; numbers in **bold** indicate charts.

DISCOVER SWEETS
FOR EVERY OCCASION
with More Books from Storey

by Valerie Peterson & Janice Fryer

Whether you want to decorate themed cookies for a baby shower, a birthday party, or a wedding, you'll find everything you need in this beautiful guide. Learn foolproof methods for rolling, baking, piping, flooding, and other key techniques.

by Sally Levitt Steinberg

Dip into the rich history of your favorite coffee companion. This pop culture–filled tribute covers everything from the origins of the donut hole to the global ascent of Krispy Kreme and includes 28 delicious donut recipes.

by Nicole Weston

Learn how easy it is to make light and smooth frozen yogurt at home! These 56 delicious flavors range from traditional to artisanal, including black cherry vanilla, chocolate malted, pistachio, and chai spice.

JOIN THE CONVERSATION. Share your experience with this book, learn more about Storey Publishing's authors, and read original essays and book excerpts at storey.com. Look for our books wherever quality books are sold or call 800-441-5700.